embroidery

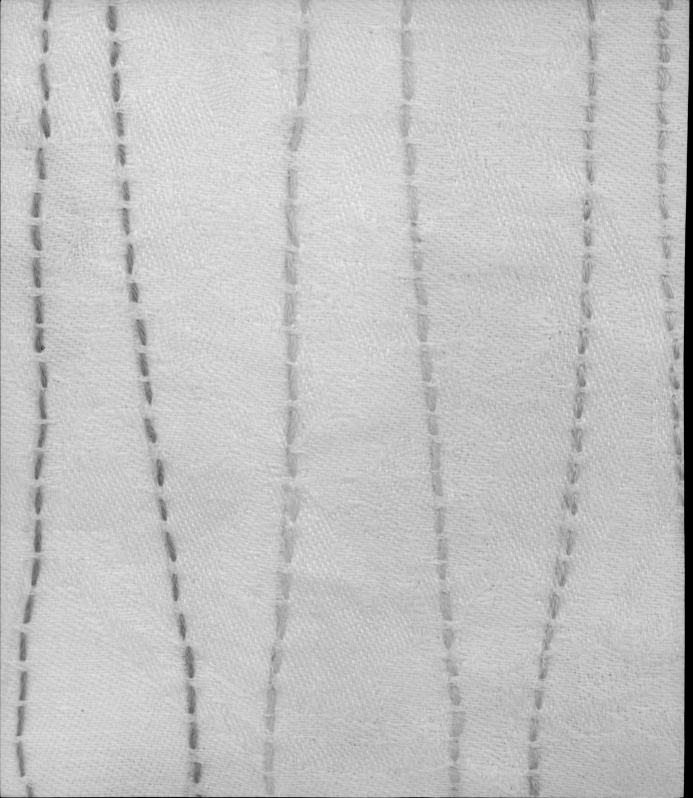

embroidery

20 projects for friends to make

super+super

First published 2014 by
Guild of Master Craftsman Publications Ltd
Castle Place, 166 High Street, Lewes,
East Sussex BN7 1XU

ISBN 978 1 86108 984 7

Publisher: Jonathan Bailey
Production Manager: Jim Bulley
Managing Editor: Gerrie Purcell
Senior Project Editor: Wendy McAngus
Editor: Sara Harper
Managing Art Editor: Gilda Pacitti
Art Editor: Rebecca Mothersole
Illustrator: Anna-Kaisa Jormanainen
Photographers: Rebecca Mothersole, Claire Culley,
Harry Watts and Kevin Meredith

Set in Akzidenz-Grotesk, Ani Lazy Day and Calibri
Colour origination by GMC Reprographics
Printed and bound in China

contents

Introduction to embroidery   8

Ready, steady, make
Using this book   12
What you'll need   14
How to do it   20

Lazy crafter
Fancy elbow pads   32
His & hers eye masks   34
Silhouette napkins   38

Weeknight winners
Glammed-up gloves   42
Geometric phone case   44
Festival shorts   48
Chill-out slippers   50

Perpetual creative
Birdhouse picture   54
Folksy bib collar   62
Vintage tray cloth curtain   66
Ikat-style cushion   70
Animal door stop   76
Cosy ear muffs   80
Wren penny purse   82
Jazzy tablet case   84

Committed crafter
Cheery banner   88
Cross-stitch chair   92
Cactus sampler   96
Stylishly stitched sweater   102
Varsity hoodie   106

Bits and bobs
Templates   112
Resources   117
Acknowledgements   118
Index   119

Introduction to embroidery

Embroidery, like many other traditional craft techniques, has very much come back into fashion over the past few years. As part of a social scene or just as a hobby at home, it's a break for many who spend their working hours staring at a computer screen. Embroidery is tactile and poses some interesting questions to distract you from the stresses of everyday life. Which colour goes with that teal floss? What combination of different stitches should you use for that picture? Should you knot the end of your floss or not?

Like drawing with a pencil we each have our own embroidery handwriting; a preferred way we make a stitch, an average stitch length, and so on. Most people have a subtle look to their style of stitching that sets that work apart from the next person. In a group of ten, no two people choose the same colours or doodle with their threads to make similar designs.

We all associate hand embroidery with specific things. Maybe it's a tablecloth from your grandparents' house, or a deliciously retro sweater, or an ornate antique wall hanging depicting some long-lost way of life or country scene. Whatever your visual inspiration may be, explore it and see what else catches your eye. We're not encouraging you to take up our slightly hoarderish tendencies, though many of the best crafters have secret stashes of glimmering buttons and jewel-coloured skeins of thread. But it is worth keeping an eye out for that certain thing that inspires you and you'll soon start to find confidence in your own personal embroidery style.

Amy & Claire, Super+Super

Get your floss out!

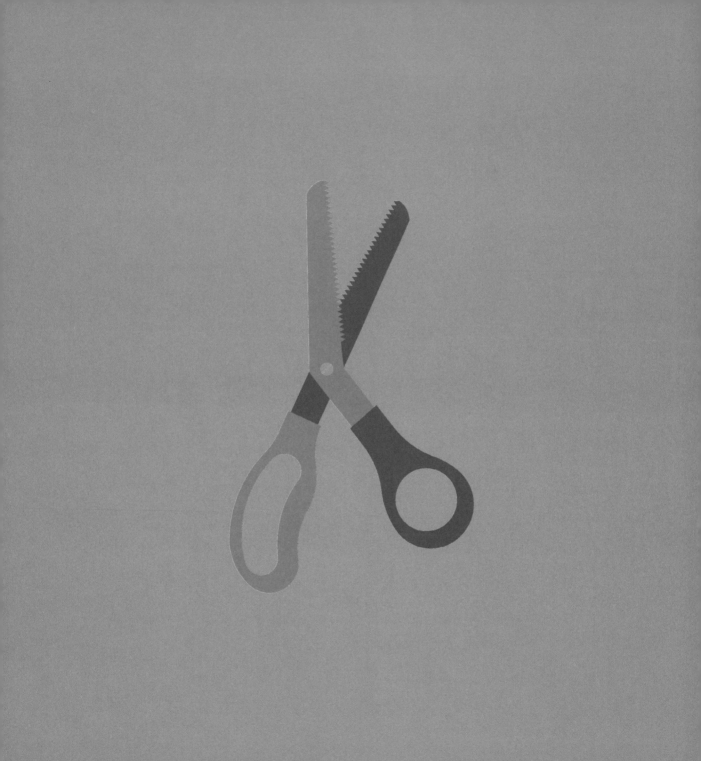

.....*(!)*.....

ready, steady, make

Using this book

Don't overwhelm yourself if embroidery is a whole new area of crafty expertise for you, but learn and master one or two techniques at a time. Try them out on different fabrics and textures and really get a feel for how they sit. Then combine them in different ways and different sizes.

Sense of colour is very personal to us all, and can change over time. Due to the fast fashion world we live in, trends in colour are ever changing too and generally we associate certain colours with different seasons and moods. The colours we have used in our projects may not be to your taste whatsoever, but fear not – once you have practised with a few examples, you will gain the confidence to work with your own colour combos and really go wild.

The care instructions for the projects in this book are pretty simple – once they are made you should keep them safe, dry and out of direct sunlight. Some threads and fabrics will fade if overexposed. Just think about how many joyful hours you have put into making that one item and cherish it!

This book is a collection of 20 projects needing varying levels of expertise. We hope you will bring your own style to each project by thrifting, reusing and swapping materials and colours. Our aim is to help the novice crafter to become a more experienced and confident designer/maker. Don't be afraid to push each project to the next level by adding and extending to a design where it appeals to you. We hope that this book inspires you to get creative and share those brilliant new skills with your friends.

This book is divided into four sections based on how long and involved a project will be. This means you can be sure you have time to finish a project before you start on it. We don't want you to end up with a half-finished project or to feel like you have to rush something.

Lazy crafter
These give you maximum impact for the minimum time and effort. These projects are great for getting you into the swing of something new or for a quick creative fix when you have only a few precious moments to spare.

Weeknight winners
These projects are short enough to be completed in a single evening after work and are often made with items readily found around a crafter's home. Great for an evening in alone or with a bunch of friends at a craft get-together.

Perpetual creative
These medium-length projects will keep you inspired over a quiet weekend (or two), giving you a creative intermission to an often hectic working week.

Committed crafter
These longer length, more complex projects can be enjoyed at your leisure over an extended period of time, holiday or sabbatical. They are perfect for building on your confidence and skills base.

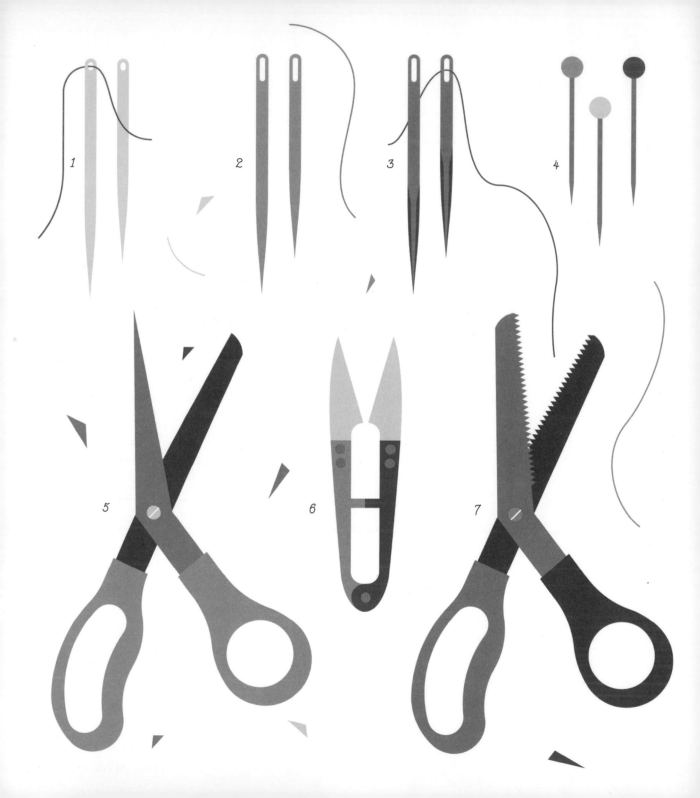

What you'll need

Tools are easy to get hold of online and in craft stores but we often pick up bits and bobs from charity shops and markets. Spend some time choosing materials for your projects from a variety of places. Some items will have to be new but maybe you could check out eBay or even organize a haberdashery swap with your friends and exchange unwanted or leftover odds and ends to inspire whole new projects without spending a single penny!

Chances are you will have almost all of the items needed for most of these projects at home. However, why not take a leaf from a thrifty maker's book and beg or borrow any additional equipment for projects you are underprepared for? As long as you return things in the same state as they were lent to you, you will be on to a winner.

By varying the age and quality of fabrics, flosses, threads and trims that you use for each project, you will achieve a really rich collection of pieces. In our projects we have tried to stick to bare essentials and thrifty alternatives that can be picked up cheaply from local haberdashery shops or online.

needles and pins

Different thicknesses of fabric need special needles. However, most projects are flexible enough for you to use your trusty favourite. It's all about how it feels and a favourite needle is generally one that has been worn in, so that it fits your fingers and works with you.

1   Sharps
These are used for general hand sewing. They have a sharp point, a round eye and are of medium length.

2   Crewels
These are standard embroidery needles, identical to sharps but with a longer eye to enable easier threading of multiple embroidery threads and thicker yarns. Try to find a needle that doesn't make large holes in your chosen fabric.

3   Leatherwork needles
These have a triangular point designed to pierce leather without tearing it, and are also often used on leather-like materials such as vinyl and plastic. Be careful – unlike a normal needle the hole this will make is irreparable.

4   Fabric pins
Dressmakers' pins, in all shapes and sizes, are essential for pinning fabrics together.

scissors and cutting utensils

5   Fabric scissors
These have a straight edge so they sit comfortably on the table when you're cutting cloth. Every crafter has their favourite pair of trusty fabric scissors. Ours are well worn and have been resharpened many times. They aren't a fancy brand but just feel good to hold and aren't too heavy. It's as much about manoeuvrability as anything.

6   Snips
These small cutters are used for trimming the ends of threads. Or you could invest in a pair of classic golden stork scissors. These dainty scissors are not cheap however, so us thrifty crafters are happy to stick with cheaper options.

7   Pinking shears
These are big heavy fabric cutting scissors with serrated blades. When you cut with these they leave a zigzag edge, which stops unwanted fraying in the blink of an eye.

miscellaneous tools

1 Paper
Ordinary paper is handy for sketching your designs and tracing templates onto.

2 Tracing paper
Any old tracing paper will do the trick when you are copying templates. Or if you can't lay your hands on that, baking parchment works well as an alternative.

3 Pencil
Again, nothing fancy is needed – just an everyday HB or 2B. We often use ours to mark the design or motif onto fabric.

Tip! Never overstretch your fabric on your embroidery hoop. It will distort the motif and alter the tension of your stitching.

4 Pen
A ballpoint or permanent marker is great for marking or adapting stencils, but will permanently mark fabric so watch out.

5 Japanese screw punch
This little device is great fun to use. It is perfect for punching holes in almost any material. Buy one online for a good deal.

6 Steel ruler
For measuring and keeping your flyaway fabrics flat and still.

7 Masking tape
Ideal for attaching templates to fabrics and then easily removable. This stuff is often unnecessarily expensive, but they sell it in all good discount stores too.

8 Embroidery hoop
Not everyone likes to work with a hoop (it comes down to personal preference), but for a couple of these projects it's essential. A hoop is actually two parts; a smaller circle that fits inside a larger one and fastens securely with an adjustable screw closure on the outer hoop.

9 Tailor's chalks
Use this to make temporary markings on fabric to show where to sew or cut. Tailor's chalk comes in several different colours and can be brushed off or washed out so it does not leave permanent marks.

10 Tape measure
A metal tape measure is always handy and is useful for quickly marking straight lines with a pencil. The fabric tailor's type is great for working around curves and pinning in place.

11 Sticky tape
The matt-finish kind in a dispenser is useful for positioning templates and even keeping stray threads in place.

12 Eraser
For rubbing out any mistakes on your templates and sketches. Nothing fancy is required – a standard school eraser will suffice.

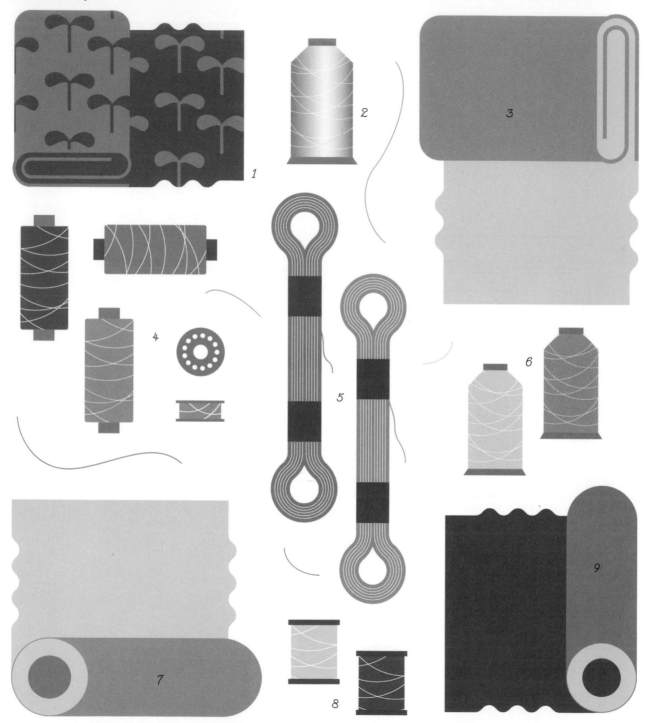

flosses, threads and fabrics

1   Damask
This is reversible fabric, usually silk or linen, with a pattern woven into it, and is most often used to make tablecloths and napkins.

2   Metallic embroidery thread/floss
This is a little more expensive than normal thread and can often fray but once you get the knack of working with it you'll love its shimmery goodness.

3   Felt
We have used wool-mix felt for our projects. It comes in a bright selection of colours and feels nicer than the synthetic type.

4   Machine thread
A spool of cotton for your sewing machine needs. Generally these are synthetic mixes unless you want to splash some cash and get the thicker, more hard-wearing, quality brands.

5   Embroidery floss
Six-stranded floss is probably the most common type of embroidery thread and the one used for most of the projects. This is made from six thin threads that are twisted together. These can be separated and used singly or a few together for finer details. It's inexpensive and comes in a huge variety of colours. It's usually 100% cotton but comes in rayon mix and silk too. Embroidery floss usually comes in little looped bundles known as skeins, secured by paper tabs to keep it untangled and the tension of the strands even. Stranded floss is colourfast so for the projects such as the elbow pads (page 32), rest assured that the dye won't bleed when you hand wash it.

6   Embroidery thread
This comes in single strands that are usually wrapped around a bobbin or card. Often more commonly associated with machine embroidery, it's tightly twisted and of a thinner quality than embroidery floss.

7   Calico
This is a plain woven fabric made from cotton and often not fully processed so it has a more rough and ready appearance. It is usually a lovely speckled creamy colour.

8   Coloured cotton threads
The thicker unstranded kind often comes in children's craft sets or the ones we have used here are from a thrift store. They have a softer worn quality, which works magic when combined with vintage fabrics.

9   Jersey and fine knits
Jersey is a fine knitted fabric that is predominantly used in clothing. It comes in a variety of different fibre contents, from wool mixes to the cotton/synthetic varieties that are more commonly used on the high street.

Tip! Always hand wash your embroidered items and don't ever put them in the washing machine.

How to do it

Use this handy guide for information on sewing a particular type of stitch in your embroidery. Most of them are fairly easy, but do try to keep your stitches all the same length for a neater look.

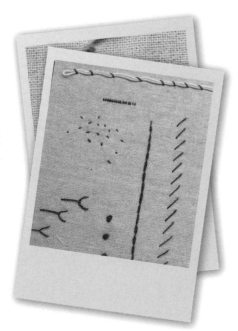

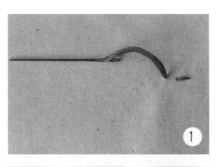

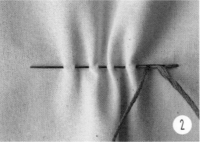

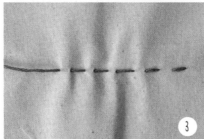

running stitch

This is the most basic stitch, so a good one to start off with.

1 Thread your needle with embroidery floss and knot the end. Stab your needle up from the back of the fabric to the front. Stab back down through the fabric a little distance to the left, then bring the point up again a little way along. Continue along like this.

2 To work faster, weave the needle through the fabric in a wave-like motion as far as you can.

3 Pull the thread through when there is no more room on the needle.

seed stitch

This is a lot like running stitch but you work the up and down wave-like motion in a freeform haphazard way.

1. Bring the needle up from the back of the fabric and then down again a small distance away.

2. Scatter lots of little stitches around in this way and don't worry too much what the back of the fabric looks like.

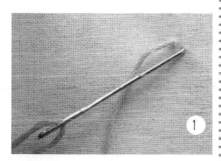

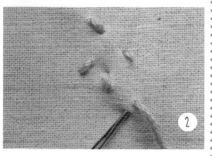

backstitch

This is a strong and flexible stitch, very good for seams.

1. Knot or secure the end of your floss and bring your needle up through your fabric from the back to the front. Take the needle back down through the fabric at point A and then back up again at point B.

2. Pull the floss through. Now take the point down very close to point C, the left-hand end of the first stitch. Bring the point of the needle back up a similar distance along from point B.

3. Continue in this way, repeating this up, backwards and through, forwards and back up again motion to get your lovely backstitch.

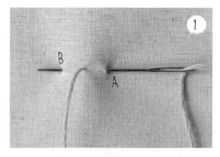

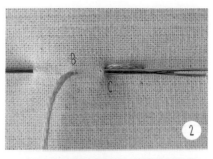

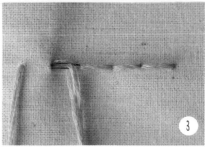

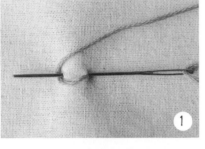
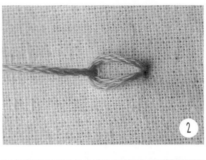
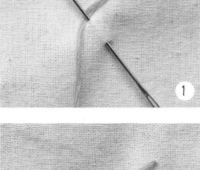

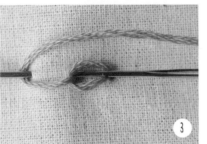
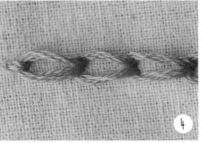
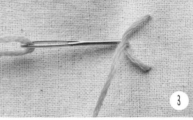

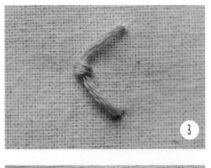

chain stitch

This pretty stitch is so useful it has inspired a whole list of variants.

1 Bring your needle up through your fabric from the back and pull the floss through. Stab the needle back into the fabric next to where it came up and push the point up a little to the left. Loop the floss under the point before you pull the floss through.

2 Do not pull the floss too tightly so that your loop lies flat on the top of the fabric.

3 Now stab the needle back in next to where it last came out and up again a similar distance along to the left, looping the floss under the point as before.

4 Repeat this sequence to make your chain as long as you want. When it is complete, finish off by securing the last chain with a small stitch.

scalloping chain stitch

This is an open version of the chain stitch, useful for borders and foliage.

1   Bring the floss up through the fabric. Now, instead of stabbing your needle back down into the fabric right next to where you started (as you would for normal chain stitch), push your needle down about ¼in (0.5cm) along. Push the point of the needle up between these two points but over to the side. Loop the floss under the needle before you pull it through.

2   Do not pull the thread taut but use your needle or finger to hold the stitch to the side, creating a little smile shape.

3   Stab your needle back down through the fabric to secure the crescent stitch you have just made.

4   Bring your needle back up next to the crescent you have made and make another stitch next to it in the same way. Continue in a line and finish neatly at the back.

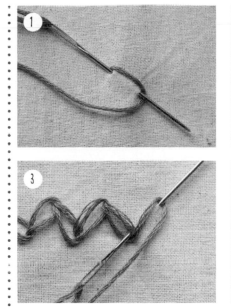

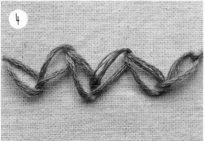

staggered chain stitch

This variation on chain stitch gives a travelling zigzag shape.

1   Pull your floss up through the fabric. Stab your needle down next to where you came up, then bring the point up again a small distance away. Loop the floss under the point before you pull the needle through. Your needle should be at a 45° angle to the direction the stitch is travelling in.

2   When you have made your first chain make the second at 45° to the first.

3   Continue along making a zigzag of chain stitches. Always pull the floss through in the direction of the loop, to keep the tension even so that the stitches lie flat on the fabric.

4   When you have made your last chain secure it with a small stitch.

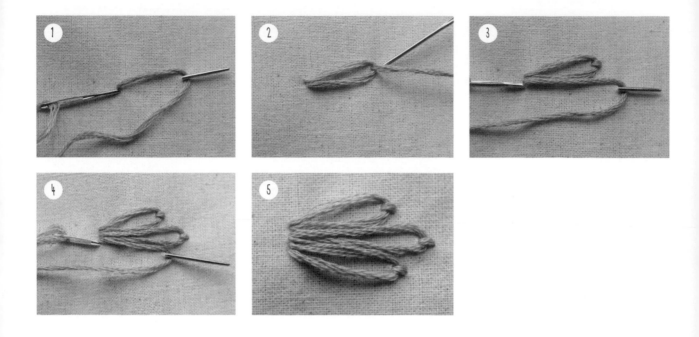

chain-stitch spray

This chain-stitch variation is perfect for leaves and floral patterns.

1 Bring the floss up through the fabric then stab your needle back down into the fabric right next to it. Push the point of the needle up in front of this and loop the floss under the needle before you pull it through.

2 Pull the floss through and make a small stitch to hold the loop in place.

3 Bring the needle back up next to the base of the chain stitch you just made. Repeat the process to make another, slightly longer chain stitch.

4 Finish the second chain off with a small stitch as before and then make another chain, the same length as the first, next to the longer chain stitch.

5 Finish off the last loop with a small stitch at the top as before.

Tip! Keep the three stitches close together at the bottom and spread further apart at the top where the loops are fastened down. This will give a great fanned out shape to the motif.

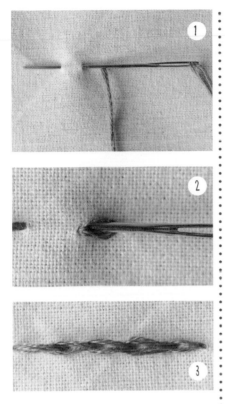

french knot

This is a wonderfully decorative stitch and can be used for securing sequins if you fancy adding sparkle to your projects.

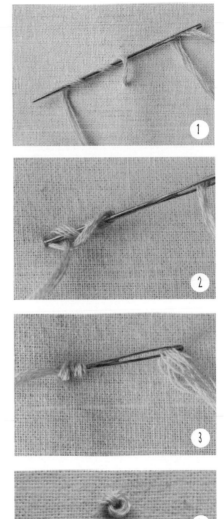

1 Secure the end of your floss and bring your needle up through the front of your fabric. Holding the point of your needle pointing to the left, wrap the length of thread away from you around the needle in an anticlockwise direction three or four times.

2 Keeping those wraps taut on your needle, push the point back down into the fabric very close to where you came up.

3 As you pull the needle down, the wraps will be gathered together.

4 Once the floss is pulled through, the wraps will be pulled down against the fabric in a sweet little knot.

split stitch

Similar to backstitch, this looks like chain stitch, but is quicker and uses less floss.

1 Bring your needle up through your fabric, then down and up again.

2 Now stab down through your first stitch, splitting the floss.

3 Continue in this way, to make a pretty chain effect.

diagonal straight stitch

This makes a nice frame or accent touch.

1 Pull thread through from the back of the fabric to the front. Imagine you have come up at the bottom left corner of a small square, and take the needle back down at the top right corner and out through the top left.

2 Now imagine another square directly above the first and stab the needle down at the top right corner of that and out through the top left.

3 Continue in this way, forming a striking column of oblique stitches.

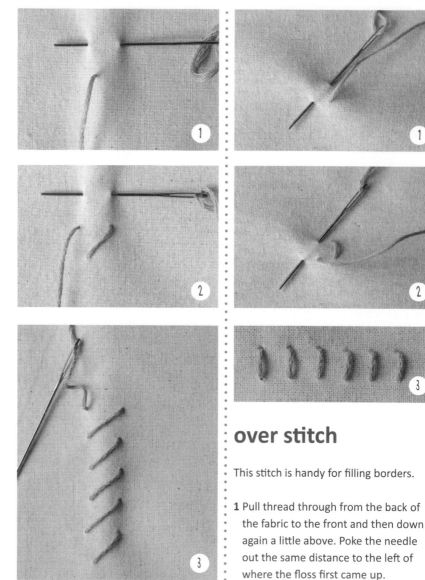

over stitch

This stitch is handy for filling borders.

1 Pull thread through from the back of the fabric to the front and then down again a little above. Poke the needle out the same distance to the left of where the floss first came up.

2 Pull the thread through and then repeat to make another vertical stitch.

3 Carry on to make a jaunty row.

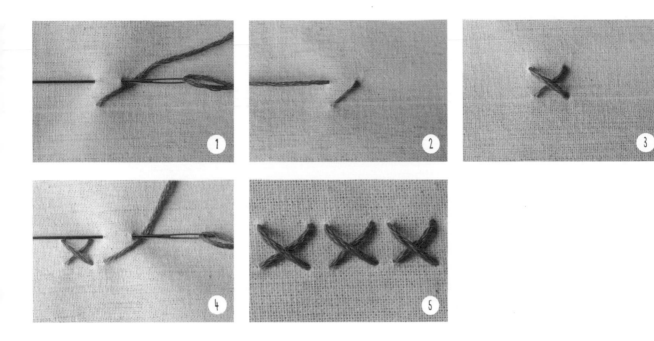

cross stitch

Cross stitch can be used for all sorts
of borders and patterns, giving a cosy
home-spun look.

1 Imagine a square that your cross will
   sit in and bring the floss up at the
   bottom left-hand corner of it. Take
   the needle back down at the top right
   corner and then out at the top left.

2 Pull the floss through.

3 Stab your needle back down through
   the fabric at the bottom right-hand
   corner of the imaginary square.

4 Bring your needle back up to the
   front of the fabric, next to where
   you finished the last stitch. Then,
   imagining a new square, take the
   needle back down at the top right
   corner and then out at the top left.

5 Stab your needle back down through
   the fabric at the bottom right-hand
   corner of the imaginary square to
   complete your second cross. Continue
   your row of stitches in this way.

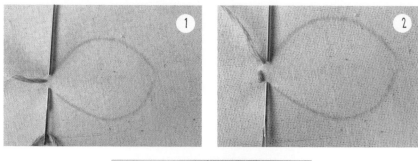

couching

Couching is where you secure a length of cord or thick floss onto fabric using a thinner thread. You can use the same colour to hide the stitching.

1 Lay your cord or floss to be couched onto the base fabric in the shape required. Having secured your thinner thread at the back of the fabric, bring your needle through to the right side of the work just below the cord.

2 Now attach the cord to the fabric by stabbing the needle into the fabric above the cord along to the right and then bringing the needle out under the cord further along.

3 Carry on along the length of the cord, anchoring the cord securely to the fabric.

4 Make sure to keep your stitches even, especially if you are using a contrasting colour of thread.

satin stitch

This is perfect for blocking in large pattern areas. You can add height to the area by filling the shape with scattered seed stitches before you start. You can also outline the shape in backstitch to add height and to use as a guideline.

1 Mark the area with tailor's chalk and bring the needle up from the back of the fabric at the edge of this area. Take your needle down at the bottom of the shape and up again at the top.

2 Stab the needle back down next to where you pushed it down before, and up again at the top. This will form a long stitch on top of the fabric.

3 Continue stabbing in at the bottom of the shape and out at the top, forming long stitches that lie next to each other. Keep your stitches close together and regular so that they lie smoothly. Fasten off your floss on the back of the work.

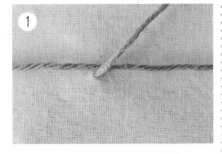

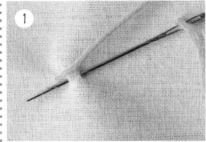

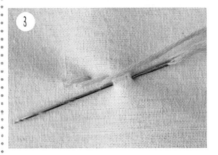

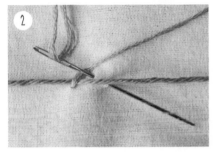

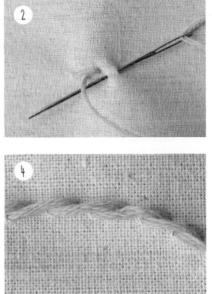

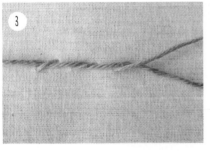

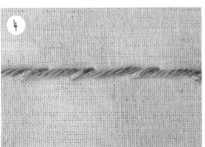

stem stitch

As its name suggests this is the perfect stitch for flower stems.

1 Bring your needle up from the back of the fabric and then down to the right, slightly above the line that you are working along. Bring the needle up again in between these two points and a little lower.

2 Repeat this sequence, travelling to the right, in a similar way to backstitch and split stitch.

3 Continue in this way with the stitches leaning on each other like roof tiles.

4 The line of stitches can be used to create a curve, making it ideal for foliage or writing. For consistency, always bring your needle up on the same side of the previous stitch.

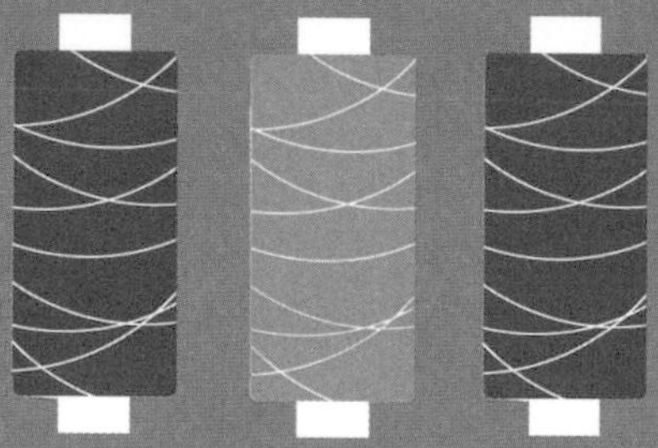

\i/:/ ! \:\i/;

lazy crafter

¿/!\:\ ¡ /:/!\¿

Fancy elbow pads

Rescue that much-loved favourite cardigan or sweater with the addition of some decorative elbow pads. It's traditional, simple and very effective. Felt is easiest to stitch but you could use leather pads, depending on your garment's style.

WHAT YOU NEED

- [ ] Old cardigan
- [ ] 8 x 8in (20 x 20cm) square of felt
- [ ] Yellow, pink and black embroidery floss
- [ ] Paper for your template
- [ ] Paper scissors
- [ ] Fabric scissors
- [ ] Pencil
- [ ] Embroidery needle
- [ ] Pins

1 Draw an oval or print out a zero in Times at 600 point and use the paper scissors to cut out the shape. Then use the fabric scissors to follow around the outline of the template and neatly cut out two elbow pads from the felt.

2 Take the first felt shape and start to customize your elbow pad. Thread the needle with a length of yellow embroidery floss approximately 24in (60cm) long and tie a knot in the very end. Bring the needle up through the elbow pad so that the knot is hidden on the inside of the pad. Chain stitch (see page 22) around the edge of the whole elbow pad. On the final stitch, turn the elbow pad over and stitch through one of the last stitches a few times to secure the end of the floss. You can also tie a knot in the end of the floss as close as possible to the pad if you prefer.

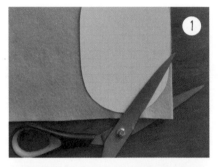

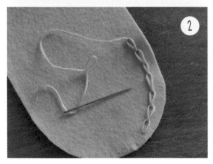

Tip! Sewing onto the cardigan can be a bit tricky. To avoid sewing the sleeve together as well, roll it up so it's easier to control.

3 Thread your needle with a length of pink embroidery floss approximately 24in (60cm) long and do the cross-stitch detailing (see page 27). Don't worry about any mess at the back of the pad as this will be covered.

4 Once you have finished your row of cross stitches, pin the elbow pad onto the cardigan.

5 Thread your needle with a 12in (30cm) length of black embroidery floss and secure the pad onto the cardigan using backstitch (see page 21). Once sewn on, repeat the steps for the second elbow pad.

His & hers eye masks

WHAT YOU NEED

☐ 2 eye masks
☐ Tailor's chalk
☐ Pink and blue embroidery floss
☐ Embroidery needle
☐ Scissors

We encourage you to nap more with this sweet stitched eye mask project. Add your own details to the masks, or you could personalize the designs to resemble your pals.

Tip! If you are not confident drawing the design yourself, trace the template onto tracing paper, then draw over the back of it so that the pencil marks transfer to the eye masks.

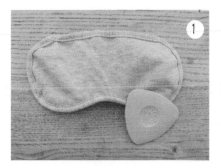

1 Draw the design onto the masks with tailor's chalk using the template (page 114) as a guide. We chose a simple sleeping eye design, but you can make yours as elaborate as you wish.

2 Cut a piece of blue embroidery floss approximately 12in (30cm) long and tie a knot in one end. Beginning with the brow, thread through from the inside of the mask to the front so that the knot is hidden. Begin to work in split stitch (see page 25) along your chalked line. Once you've reached the end of the brow, stitch over the last stitch a few times on the underneath of the mask to secure it.

3 Repeat the same stitch for the closed eye and then add eyelashes in running stitch (see page 20).

4 Repeat steps 1–3 for the second eye to complete the design.

5 Using the pink embroidery floss, repeat steps 1–4 to embroider the second eye mask.

CHILL-OUT SLIPPERS, PAGE 50

FANCY ELBOW PADS, PAGE 32

Silhouette napkins

WHAT YOU NEED

- [ ] Plain fabric napkins
- [ ] Embroidery needle
- [ ] Light blue, yellow and pink embroidery floss
- [ ] Pencil
- [ ] Fork, knife and spoon

This playful design is perfect for any dinner party. We have used vintage linen napkins handed down from a relative but you can find this type of plain damask in most charity shops or at second-hand markets.

1   Place your napkin on a flat surface. Lay out your fork, knife and spoon on the far right-hand corner and lightly pencil around them.

2   Cut a length of light blue embroidery floss approximately 24in (60cm) long and tie a knot in the end. Thread your needle with the floss and, using the pencil mark as a guide, bring the needle up through the napkin so that the knot is hidden. Start to sew around the spoon outline using a simple running stitch (see page 20).

3   Once you reach the end of the spoon, bring the needle down through the napkin and fasten the last stitch with a knot on the reverse side.

4   Thread your needle with a length of yellow embroidery floss and repeat steps 2 and 3 to embroider the knife outline.

5   Thread your needle with the final colour of floss and repeat steps 2 and 3 to embroider the fork outline.

Tip! There's no need to have a matching set of napkins — a mismatched collection looks fantastic with this bright motif.

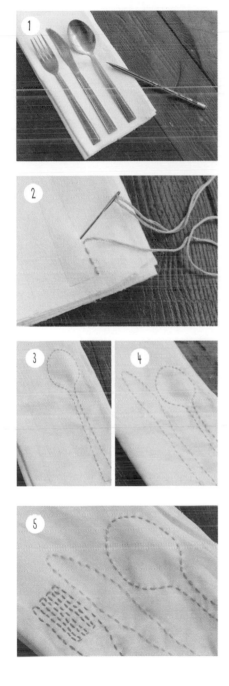

(' . . . weeknight winners . . . ,)

Glammed-up gloves

Simple and effective, this short project is great for an autumnal evening and for mastering that oh-so-simple-looking, yet just slightly tricky French knot stitch. The pattern here consists of a French knot followed by, and connected to, a running stitch.

WHAT YOU NEED

☐ Pair of knitted or fabric gloves
☐ Pink, burgundy and yellow wool tapestry thread
☐ Embroidery needles
☐ Small scissors

1 Thread your needle with a length of pink tapestry thread approximately 12in (30cm long) and tie a knot in the end of the thread. Turn the cuff of the glove over a little so you can start sewing from the inside, hiding the knot. Bring the needle through to the front of the glove and then put the point back in right next to where it came up.

2 Hold the tapestry wool taut and wrap around the needle four times to make a good-sized knot. Without letting go of the wool, go back down through to the inside of the glove, slipping the needle through the wraps to form a knot. Bring the needle back up onto the surface of the glove a little further down the glove from your French knot (see page 25).

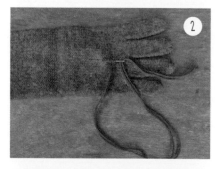

3 Now weave up and down approximately 12 times down the length of the glove and finish with the thread on the inside. Tie off your thread.

4 Repeat steps 1–3 on either side of your original line of stitches, staggering the knots and running stitches to create a woven-looking placement. Then with the burgundy thread repeat the process in between an outer line and the central one.

5 Finish with another French knot and line of stitches in yellow on the other side of the central line.

Tip! Once you've mastered the technique, why not go crazy with those French knots? More is definitely merrier.

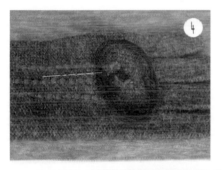

Geometric phone case

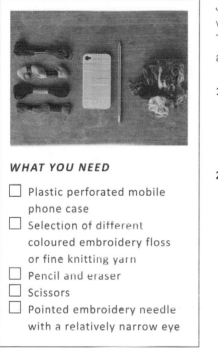

Jazz up your mobile phone case with some bold statement stitching. This is a great little project for a well-deserved night in.

1   Using the pencil, mark out the triangle pattern onto the front of your case. Follow the template shown in the picture if you like.

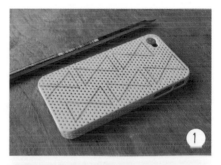

2   Thread the needle with your chosen colour thread, making sure it's no longer than your arm, and tie a knot in the very end. Starting at the point or base of the shape sew up through the case from the inside out – this will hide any unsightly tangles! Now sew back and forth, keeping the long stitches on the top side of the case following your triangle shape.

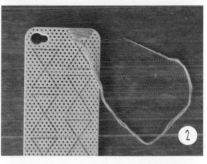

3   When you've completed your first triangle, push the needle through one of the small stitches on the back of the case.

WHAT YOU NEED

- ☐ Plastic perforated mobile phone case
- ☐ Selection of different coloured embroidery floss or fine knitting yarn
- ☐ Pencil and eraser
- ☐ Scissors
- ☐ Pointed embroidery needle with a relatively narrow eye

Tip! Snip the thread close to the knot and use a spot of superglue or clear nail polish to stick the knot down.

4 Finish the ends on the inside of the case by sewing over a few times into the back/loop of a previous stitch.

5 Using as many random or tonal colours as desired, embroider triangles all over the case.

6 Keep going until you have added as many triangles as you wish, then you're ready to click your new case onto the back of your phone for some everyday brightness.

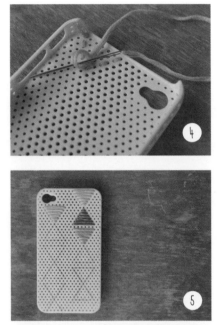

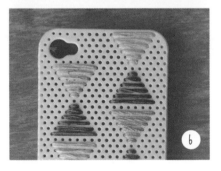

Tip! This is a great project for using up all those short bits of thread and odds and ends of floss left over from other projects.

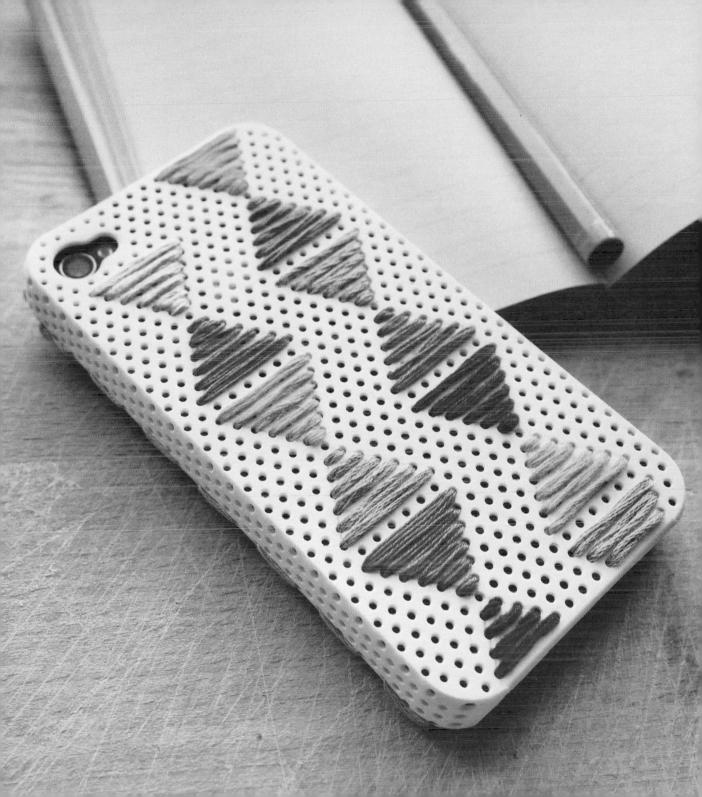

Festival shorts

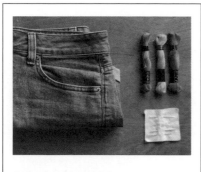

WHAT YOU NEED

☐ Pair of denim shorts
☐ Orange, turquoise and pink embroidery floss
☐ Embroidery needle
☐ Scissors

Perfect for any summer outfit, this cross-stitch upcycle project is a great way to add a cheeky detail to dull denim. Why not play with colours to complement the rest of your summer wardrobe?

1 Thread the needle with a length of the orange embroidery floss approximately 24in (60cm) long and tie a knot in the very end. Starting at the bottom corner of a pocket, working from the inside out so that the knot is hidden, take the needle through the fabric and do your first cross stitch (see page 27).

2 Repeat the cross stitch along the line of the pocket, keeping the spacing as even as possible between each one. When you reach the top, finish the end off on the inside of the pocket by sewing over a few times into the back/loop of a previous stitch. Snip off the end of the floss, leaving a small 'tail'.

3 Thread the needle with a length of turquoise embroidery floss and repeat steps 1 and 2, starting approximately 3/16 in (5mm) below the first cross-stitch line.

4 Thread the needle with the final colour of embroidery thread and repeat steps 1–2. You will end up with three lines of different coloured cross stitches. Repeat steps 1–4 to embroider the other pocket.

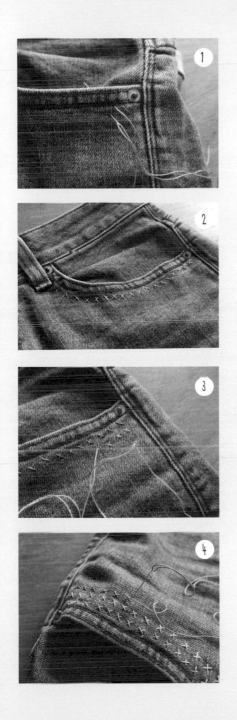

Tip! The colour choice of embroidery floss is up to you. Just go with something vibrant!

Chill-out slippers

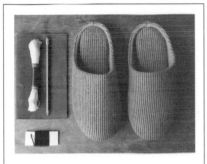

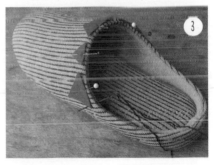

Use brightly contrasting coloured felts to get the best out of this delicate hand appliqué project. This makes a great seasonal gift idea to showcase your newly found stitching skills.

1 Draw three 1in (2.5cm) and two ½in (1.2cm) equilateral triangles on a piece of paper and cut out to use as templates. Then use fabric scissors to cut out six larger and four smaller triangle shapes from the felt.

2 Pin the felt shapes along the top of the slippers, alternating the sizes and making sure they lie flat.

3 Thread the needle with a length of embroidery floss approximately 12in (30cm) long and tie a knot at the end.

4 Sew from the inside out and, using a simple running stitch (see page 20), sew along and around all the felt pieces, appliquéing them securely to the slipper base.

5 Secure the floss end on the inside of the slipper by sewing a few times into the back of a previous stitch. Snip off the end close to these stitches.

WHAT YOU NEED

- [ ] Pair of fabric or felt slippers
- [ ] 8 x 8in (20 x 20cm) square of coloured felt
- [ ] Black embroidery floss
- [ ] Sharp embroidery needle
- [ ] Pins
- [ ] Paper scissors
- [ ] Fabric scissors

Tip! Add a scattering of French knots (see page 25) over the front of the foot for added interest if you fancy a little more stitchery.

* < * > *

perpetual creative

* < * > *

Birdhouse picture

WHAT YOU NEED

- ☐ 8in (20cm) embroidery hoop
- ☐ 12 x 12in (30 x 30cm) square piece of calico
- ☐ Black, yellow, turquoise and purple embroidery floss (or any colours that complement your appliqué fabric)
- ☐ Small piece of coloured fabric, at least 4in (10cm)
- ☐ Fabric scissors
- ☐ Embroidery needle
- ☐ Pins
- ☐ Pencil
- ☐ Superglue

In this project we take some basic steps into freehand appliqué. It may be a little fiddly but this self-framed picture project is well worth the effort. It's a great chance to play around with colours or you might want to add a twist with patterned fabric.

1 Undo the screw pin on the outside of the hoop and separate it into two parts. Position the calico over the inner hoop as centrally as possible and then replace the outside hoop on top, making the fabric stretch and become taut.

2 With fabric scissors, cut a rough square from your coloured fabric approximately 4in (10cm) and place it on top of the calico as centrally as possible. Pin at each corner.

3 With a pencil, draw two sloping lines across the top corners of your coloured fabric, to mark where the birdhouse roof will go. Thread your needle with a length of black embroidery floss approximately 12in (30cm) long and tie a knot in the end. Working from the centre point at the top of the roof, pull the thread through the calico from the back to the front.

4 Using stem stitch (see page 29), work down the right-hand side of the roof and work a couple of stitches beyond the edge of coloured fabric.

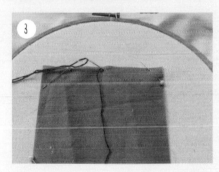

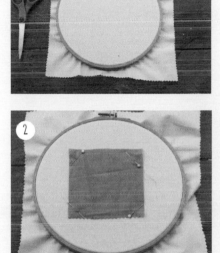

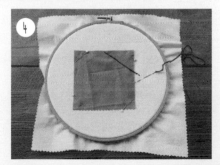

Tip! In a row of cross stitches, the top stitch should always lie in the same direction for extra neatness.

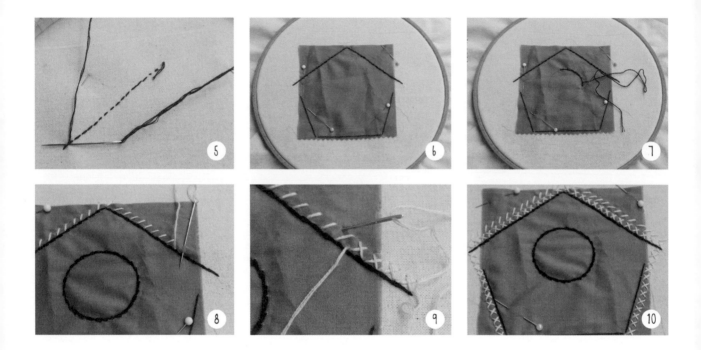

Tip! Maintain a firm but not overly tight
fabric tension throughout the project to
keep your stitches as even as possible.

5 Finish the thread neatly on the back of the work.

6 Making sure the top fabric has not wrinkled, still using stem stitch, work down from the centre point on the top of the roof to the left. Adjust the appliqué fabric as you go if it starts to crease or pucker. Then do three long running stitches (see page 20) to form the walls and base of your birdhouse.

7 Draw a circle for the birdhouse entrance with a pencil. Use a cup or jar as a guide to draw around. Using stem stitch, neatly embroider the circle in black.

8 Thread your needle with a length of yellow embroidery floss around 12in (30cm) long and tie a knot in the end. Working from bottom left to top right and across the length of your roof, pull the thread through the calico from the back to the front and stitch a line of diagonal straight stitches (see page 26).

9 Work back in the opposite direction, placing second diagonal straight stitches over the existing ones to form crosses. Finish and tie the thread off neatly at the back of your work.

10 Now, in whichever direction is easiest for you, work a row of cross stitch all the way around the black outline of the birdhouse.

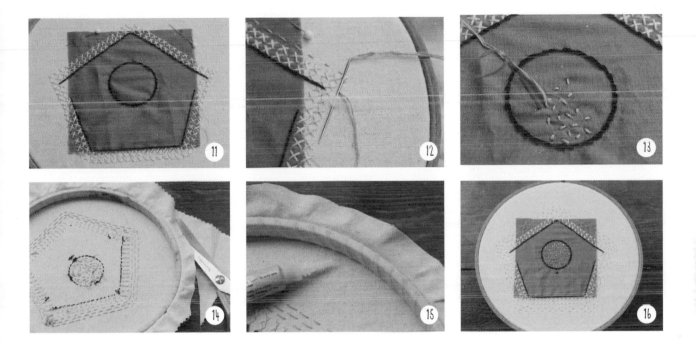

11 Repeat another row of crosses all round your birdhouse.

12 Thread your needle with a length of turquoise embroidery floss about 12in (30cm) long and tie a knot in the end. Starting at the top of the roof, pull the thread through the calico from the back to the front. Sew running stitches evenly around the cross-stitch border. Repeat this twice so there are three rows of running stitches all together.

13 Finally change to your last coloured floss and thread your needle with a length of embroidery floss that is approximately 4in (10cm) long and tie a knot in the end. Starting in the centre of the circle, pull the thread through the fabric from the back to the front and sew in seed stitches (see page 21) haphazardly until the whole area is filled.

14 Turn the hoop over and trim off any excess calico fabric, leaving a generous ¾in (2cm) border.

15 Being careful not to get any on the back of the design, dab a thin line of superglue around the inside of the wooden embroidery hoop, folding the fabric edge in to stick it firmly as you go round.

16 To finish off, add one small cross stitch (see page 27) in black under the circle to represent a perch.

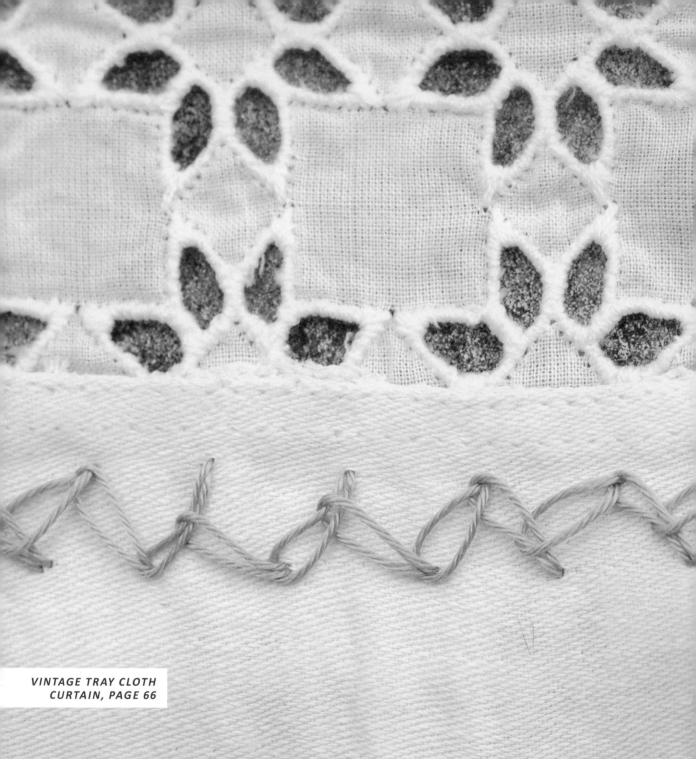

VINTAGE TRAY CLOTH CURTAIN, PAGE 66

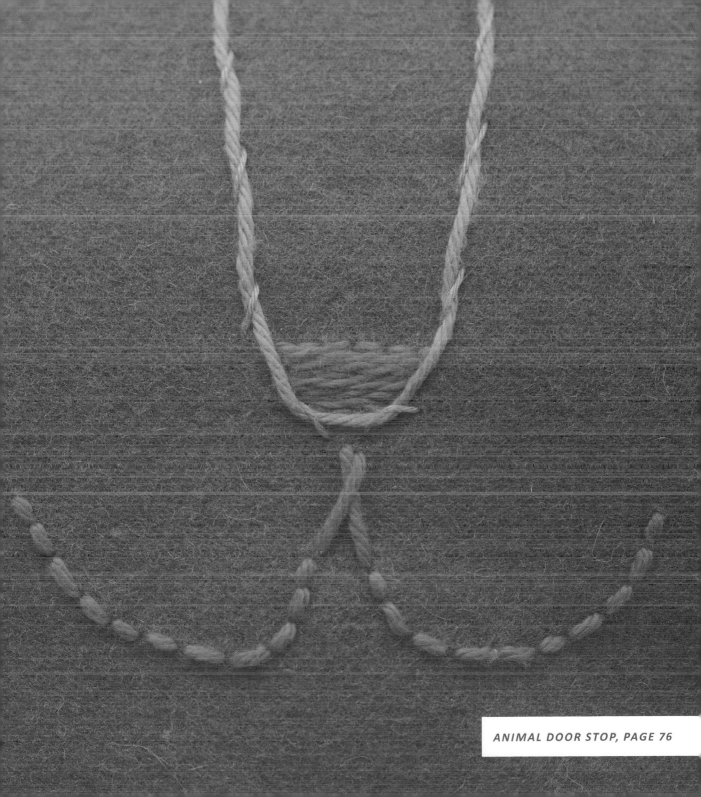

ANIMAL DOOR STOP, PAGE 76

Folksy bib collar

WHAT YOU NEED

- [ ] Plain shirt with a wide collar
- [ ] Sharp and embroidery needle
- [ ] Black embroidery floss and suitably folksy coloured threads
- [ ] Fabric scissors
- [ ] Pinking shears
- [ ] Thread in a similar colour to the shirt
- [ ] Tailor's chalk or pencil
- [ ] Pins

This chic bib collar project started off as a man's formal shirt and is an easy way to update your look without breaking the bank. Simple small stitches work to great effect on this design. Why not try teaming with a cardigan for daytime or a tailored jacket for a cool evening look?

1 Using tailor's chalk or pencil, draw the desired bib shape onto the front of the shirt. Remember to add a ⅝in (1.5cm) seam allowance as well and draw that in with the chalk or pencil.

2 Using pinking shears, cut the bib shape away from the main shirt body. Start at the front and work around to the back.

3 On the curve at the bottom of the bib, snip V-shaped notches out of the seam allowance. This will help to form a smooth line on the right side of the work when you fold the seam allowance under.

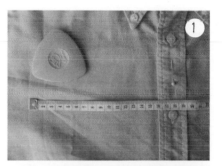

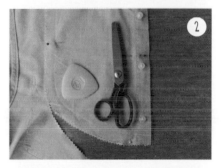

Tip! Change the buttons to vintage or brightly coloured ones for an extra special detail.

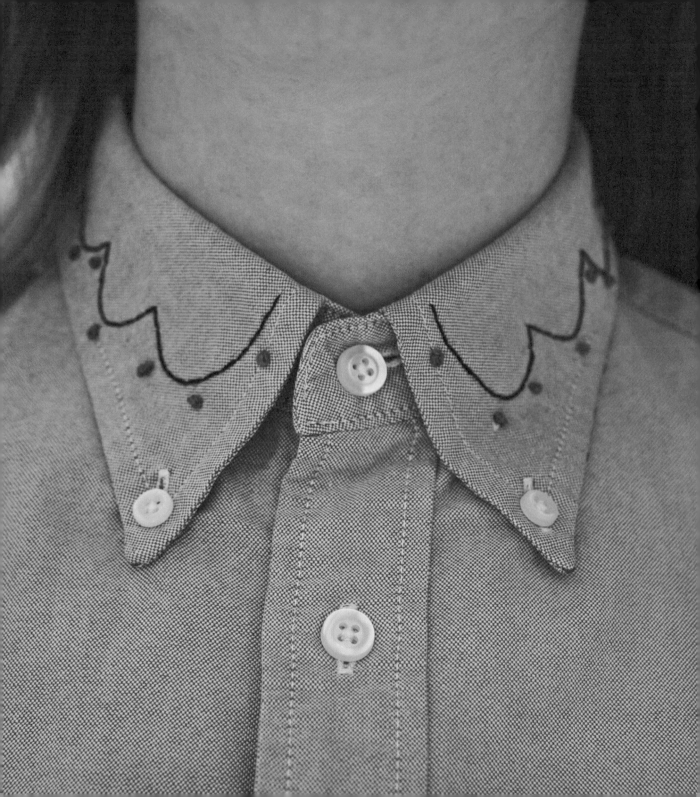

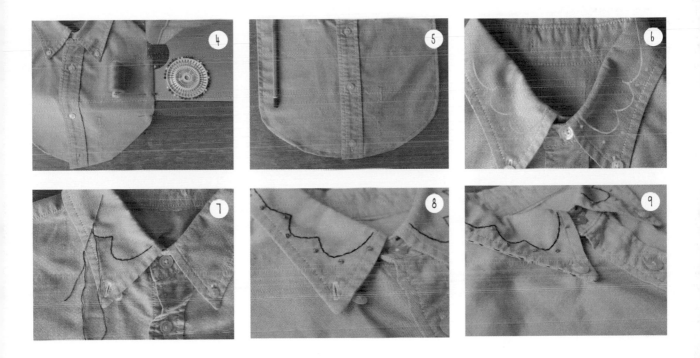

4 Fold the fabric under at the marked seam allowance, pressing with an iron if desired. Now pin.

5 Using a thread in a similar colour to the fabric of your bib, stitch all the way around the edge in backstitch (see page 21). If you have a sewing machine it's much easier. Tie the threads off on the back of the bib so they are out of sight.

6 Now draw the motif onto your collar freehand using tailor's chalk or trace the template (see page 112) and transfer it to the collar by drawing over it on the back to transfer the pencil marks.

7 Let the embroidery begin! Thread up your needle with a length of black embroidery floss approximately 24in (60cm) long and knot at the end. Follow the curved line in simple running stitch (see page 20).

8 Thread up your needle with a length of coloured embroidery floss and add French knots (see page 25) below the curves.

9 Finally, using a bright-coloured thread, sew a cheeky running stitch into the seam edge of the collar.

Tip! Cutting triangular notches around curved edges allows hems to fold over neatly and easily.

Vintage tray cloth curtain

WHAT YOU NEED

- [ ] Selection of different-sized tray cloths
- [ ] Embroidery threads in various colours
- [ ] Sharp-ended embroidery needles
- [ ] Pins
- [ ] Filler fabric such as broderie anglaise or lace
- [ ] Tape measure
- [ ] Small scissors

Definitely one of our more feminine projects, this tea cloth curtain is a vintage textiles hoarder's dream. The more contrasting fabric and textures you can combine, the better! Keep an eye out for original embroidery to add an extra playful twist. Don't be afraid to cut up even really old cloths and liners as it's better these pieces are being displayed and loved than stashed away in a box out of sight.

1   Measure the width and height of your chosen window and decide how big you want your curtain to be. Lay your chosen tray cloths out and fit them together in the way you think looks best. Space the cloths out within the area that the curtain will take up, using your tape measure to help you. Allow a small overlap between each one. Now cut pieces of your filler fabric big enough to fill any spaces between your tray cloths. Once it's all fitting together nicely, pin the fabrics together. You'll need a lot of pins!

2   You can now begin to sew simple embroidery stitches, such as running stitch (see page 20) to join your pieces together.

Tip! You might want to tack pieces together with a running stitch for extra security before you start using fancy stitches.

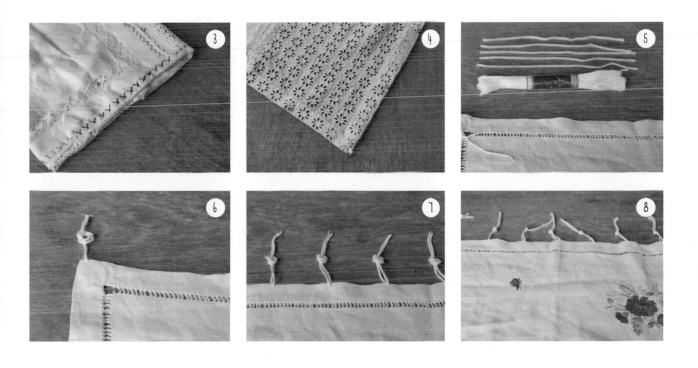

3 On our curtain we have used
running stitch, cross stitch (page 27),
staggered chain stitch (page 23) and
diagonal straight stitch (page 26)
in different coloured embroidery
threads to join the cloths. You can
use your favourite stitches in all one
colour of thread if you prefer.

4 Once your panels are securely joined
together, hem any rough or cut edges.

5 Using either a thick cotton thread
or an embroidery thread, cut lots of
same-sized lengths approximately 8in
(20cm) long. These will become your
curtain loops for hanging the panel.

6 Thread a length onto a needle and
push it through the cloth at the top
corner of your curtain. Remove the
needle and now loosely knot the two
ends of the threads together.

7 Continue along the top of the curtain,
spacing the threads approximately 2in
(5cm) apart. Do not tighten the knots.

8 Once you have attached all the
threads to the top of the curtain and
you are happy with their placement,
tighten the knots. Press your panel
before hanging.

Ikat-style cushion

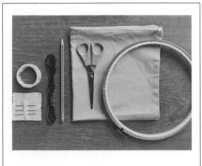

WHAT YOU NEED

- [ ] Plain cushion cover
- [ ] Red and yellow embroidery floss
- [ ] Embroidery needle
- [ ] Tape measure
- [ ] Pencil
- [ ] 8in (20cm) embroidery hoop
- [ ] Scissors

This two-colour project is inspired by the current trend for all things graphic, plus the traditional Ikat style of weaving. Play around with different colour combos to change the look – but bright is definitely best.

1   Mark out your grid on the bottom right-hand side of your cushion cover. To do this, measure 1in (2.5cm) from the right of your cushion and lay your tape vertically. Then mark a dot at every inch (2.5cm) for 8in (20cm).

2   Move the tape measure another inch (2.5cm) to the left and mark another eight dots. Repeat this until you have five lines of dots as shown.

3   Separate the embroidery hoop into two parts. Unzip your cushion and pop the top side of the cushion over the inner hoop, then replace the outside hoop on top and tighten. Make sure you have access to inside your cushion as you'll be sewing only onto the top. Thread your needle with a length of red embroidery floss approximately 36in (90cm) long. Starting at the far right of the grid from the inside of the cushion cover, pull the thread through to the front and sew a diagonal line about 1¼in (3cm) long as shown.

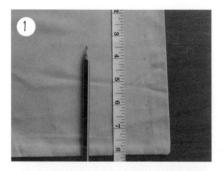

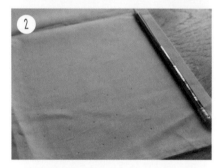

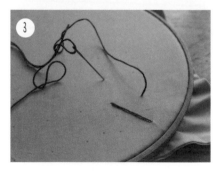

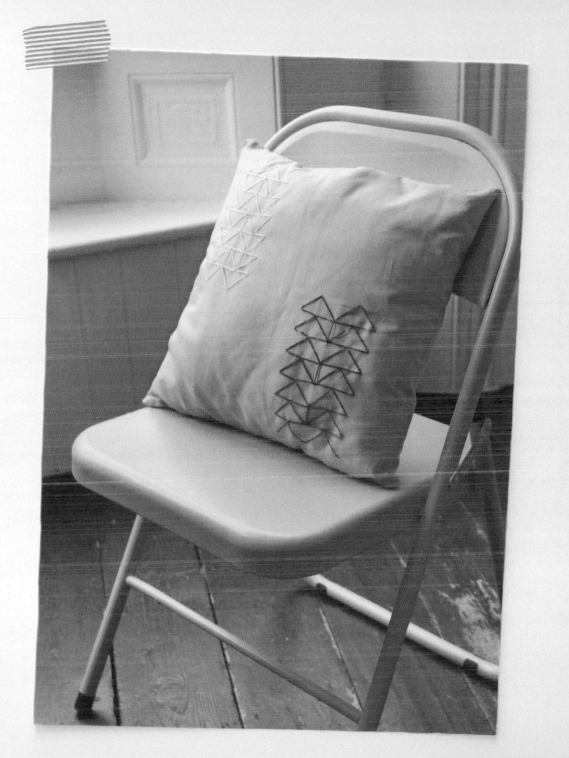

4 Continue to sew diagonal straight stitches (see page 26) about 1¼in (3cm) long in a column.

5 When you reach the top of the grid, sew the horizontal lines back down as shown to create a zigzag effect.

6 Repeat the same steps on the next grid column to form a mirror image to your first line of stitches.

7 Now sew two more columns of diagonal straight stitches to form a horizontal chevron.

8 Next, it's time to sew the small horizontal lines the same as the opposite edge.

9 Carry on until you have completed all the lines in that column.

10 When you reach the last horizontal stitch, come straight back up and do one long stitch over to the horizontal stitch opposite it. Then come up one grid dot higher and repeat in the other direction.

11 Continue in this way up to the top of the grid. When you reach the top of the design, come up in the centre and sew a vertical stitch over one row of the grid. Repeat this on every other grid line.

12 Turn the cushion cover upside down and repeat the same design in yellow embroidery floss in the opposite corner.

Tip! Turn your cushion over and decorate the back as well if you fancy introducing more colours into your world.

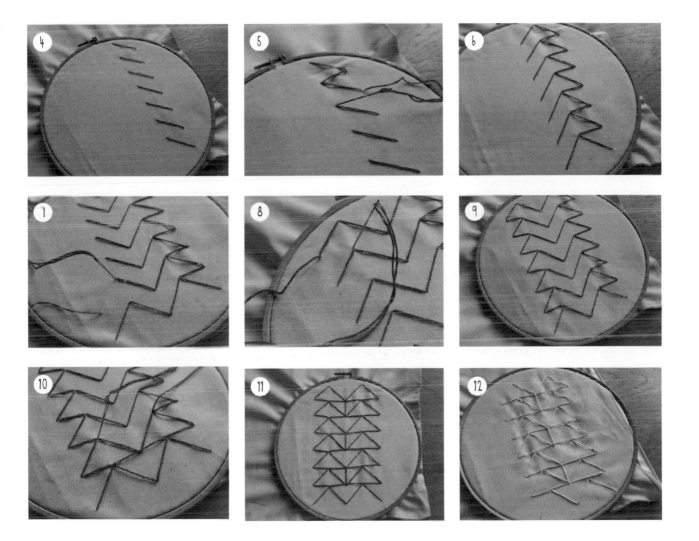

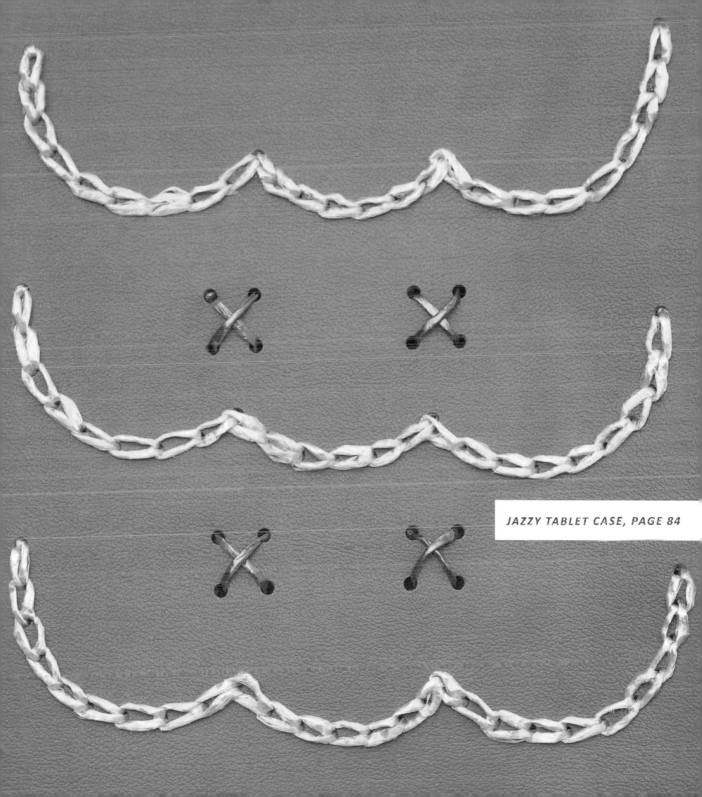

JAZZY TABLET CASE, PAGE 84

Animal door stop

WHAT YOU NEED

- ☐ Plate, approximately 8in (20cm) in diameter
- ☐ Tailor's chalk
- ☐ Thick fabric
- ☐ Pinking shears
- ☐ Embroidery floss in pink, light blue and dark blue
- ☐ Machine thread in light blue (to use as couching thread)
- ☐ Sewing machine
- ☐ Needle
- ☐ White rice
- ☐ Toy stuffing
- ☐ Pins
- ☐ Scissors

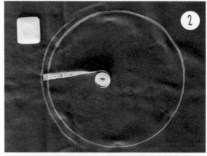

Inspired by the many plush needlework projects of the 1970s, our feline friend is a great project for mastering the couching technique. We have used scraps of upholstery fabric to toughen this fellow up, but you could just use any standard nice quality wool mix felt.

1 Using a side plate as your template, mark out two circular pattern pieces on your chosen base fabric with tailor's chalk.

2 Add an extra ⅝in (1.5cm) seam allowance for hemming.

3 Cut both the pieces out using a pair of pinking shears. Keep the remnants to make the cat's ears. Select the colours of floss you are going to use.

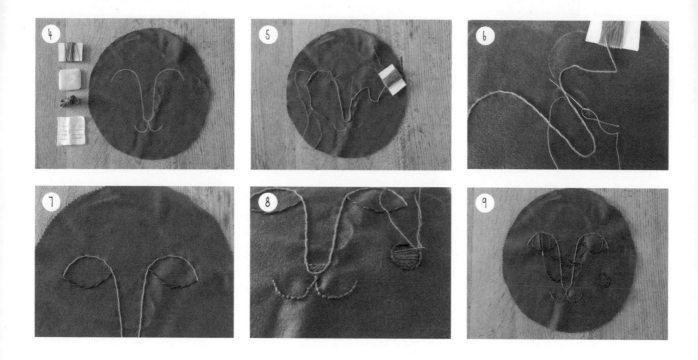

4 Trace the template of the cat's face onto tracing paper (see page 116) and copy it onto one of the circles by drawing over it on the back to transfer the pencil marks. Make it clearer to follow using tailor's chalk.

5 Lay your light blue embroidery floss on top of the fabric and, using your needle, sew the end through the fabric and knot at the back. Do the same with your thinner couching thread so they both start very close together. Pin down along the length of your thicker thread to keep it flat and the tension even.

6 Working in one direction, couch along the length of the thick thread, taking time to navigate curves neatly by adding more stitches where necessary (see page 28). Try to keep your stitches evenly spaced. Sew the thread through to the back of the fabric when you come to the end of the motif and fasten off by sewing over a couple of times.

7 Repeat this process with dark blue embroidery floss for the bottom of the eyes, bearing in mind it may be a little more fiddly as the thread is much shorter.

8 Change to pink embroidery floss and use a backstitch (see page 21) to sew on the mouth detail. Couch on a small circle with the dark blue embroidery floss. Fill this with satin stitch (see page 28) in pink embroidery floss, and then the tip of the nose in the same way.

9 Use a very thin strand of light blue embroidery floss to sew running stitch (see page 20) for the circular eye detail. Then sew a single chain stitch (see page 22) in dark blue embroidery floss for the pupil.

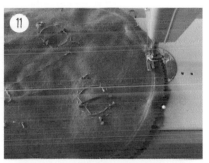

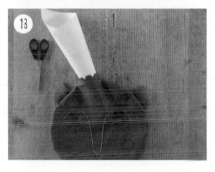

Tip! Experiment with different fabrics and animal faces to create a whole door-stop menagerie for your home.

10 Use long running stitch to add a couple of whiskers and then turn the cat face over. Place on top of the other circle of fabric so that the right sides are together. Pin in place. Cut two ear-shaped pieces from your leftover fabric and lay them on top of the circles to decide where they look best. Once you've decided, pin the ear pieces in position.

11 Using backstitch or a sewing machine, carefully sew around the edge of your pinned shapes, leaving an opening at the top between the ears for stuffing. Snip into the seam allowance all around the edge at regular intervals.

12 Turn the door stop the right way and get ready to stuff!

13 Pour approximately 7oz (200g) rice into the bottom of your cat cushion to give it weight. Use a sheet of paper and tape to make a funnel so it's easy to pour the rice into your door stop.

14 Fill the rest of the shape with synthetic toy stuffing until your door stop has the desired plumpness. Pin the top closed and then hand stitch together with a running or over stitch.

Cosy ear muffs

This is a fun project for textile lovers to get their teeth into. Take time in building up the layers of different stitches to achieve a really bold motif inspired by Mexican tapestries.

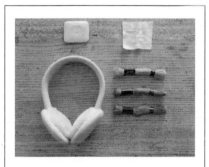

WHAT YOU NEED

- ☐ Pair of woven or fabric-covered ear muffs
- ☐ Tailor's chalk or pencil
- ☐ Blue, green and orange embroidery threads
- ☐ Embroidery needle
- ☐ Scissors

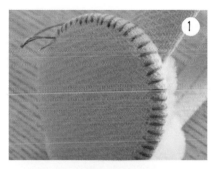

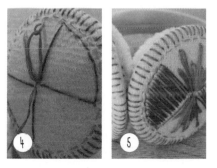

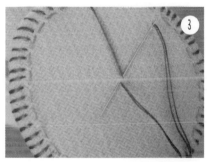

1 Thread your needle with a length of blue embroidery thread that is approximately 12in (30cm) long. Knot the thread at the end and start the first stitch on the inside of the ear muffs so as to hide the knot in the fluffy lining. Stitch all around the edge in blue embroidery thread in over stitch (see page 26).

2 Now follow the template (page 113), either by eye or by marking it onto the fabric with tailor's chalk or a soft pencil. Thread your needle with green embroidery thread approximately 12in (30cm) long and using running stitch (see page 20) sew a line under your stitches on the outer edge. Finish the ends on the underside of the ear muff by sewing over a few times into the back of a previous stitch.

3 The central motif area is divided into four quadrants. Use four long running stitches to divide the area up.

4 Define the edge of two opposite quadrants with backstitch (see page 21), just under the green running stitch. Using a length of orange embroidery thread approximately 12in (30cm) long fill the other two quadrants with a chain-stitch spray (see page 24).

5 Using blue thread and a relaxed satin stitch (see page 28) so that the stitches are not flush together, fill in the two empty quadrants.

Wren penny purse

WHAT YOU NEED

- [ ] Leather or faux leather coin purse
- [ ] Gold embroidery thread and two other colours that complement the colour of the purse you have chosen
- [ ] Silver pen
- [ ] Leatherwork needles
- [ ] Tracing paper

This petite project may prove a challenge for a few but is definitely worth its weight in golden stitches. The leather of the purse gives a whole different surface texture to work on and a leather needle is definitely an essential. Take care not to stab your surface too haphazardly as this needle will cut through even the toughest hide, causing irreparable holes.

1 Trace the template (see page 112) onto tracing paper, then transfer to the purse by drawing over the back of the design so that pencil marks transfer to the purse. Draw over in silver pen.

2 Split a length of the thread you have chosen for the bird in half and thread it onto your leatherwork needle. Tie a knot at the end and push the needle through the leather from the inside of the purse.

3 In varying lengths of backstitch (see page 21) stitch the bird design, starting with the outline. Finish off neatly on the inside of the purse by sewing over the stitch a few times.

4 With the second coloured thread, again split the thread in half, and use backstitch to fill in the lettering.

5 Next, using one strand of the gold thread, do a French knot (see page 25) for the bird's eye

6 Add gold stitches to highlight the feathers and beak, then backstitch a circle around the bird.

7 Finish with small seed stitches (see page 21) dotted evenly around the outer edge of the circle.

Jazzy tablet case

Keep your tablet as safe as houses while you dazzle your friends with some bold stitching. This is a mixed media project that will be difficult to miss. All materials were sourced from discount stores, proving that style does not have to break the bank.

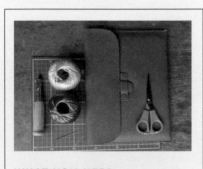

WHAT YOU NEED

- [ ] Faux leather tablet case
- [ ] Pencil
- [ ] Cutting mat
- [ ] Japanese hole punch
- [ ] Pink and yellow plastic raffia string
- [ ] Small scissors
- [ ] Round-ended embroidery needle

Tip! If you are not confident about drawing the design, you can trace it onto tracing paper and then put it pencil side down on the case before drawing over the back to transfer the pattern.

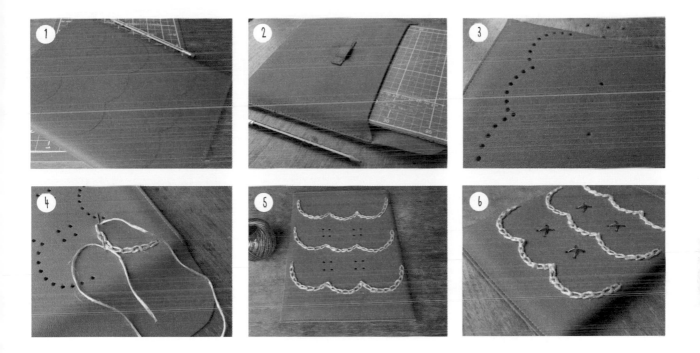

1. Using a soft pencil, copy the pattern from page 115 onto the surface of your tablet case.

2. Slot a cutting mat inside the case.

3. Using a medium pressure, punch out holes with the Japanese hole punch at ½in (1.3cm) intervals along the curves and at each corner of the crosses. Remove the cutting mat.

4. Take a 24in (60cm) length of yellow plastic raffia string, thread it on your needle and knot the end. Push the needle through the case, sewing from the inside out so that the knot is hidden. Using chain stitch (see page 22), sew along the punched-out curve part of the design.

5. Knot the thread inside the case when you come to the end of the line. Repeat this twice more.

6. Thread your needle with a 12in (30cm) length of pink plastic raffia string and knot the end. Push the needle through the case in one of the top holes in the groups of four, sewing from the inside out. Sew the two top cross stitches (see page 27) into the top pair of four punched holes. Finish the thread off on the inside of the case then repeat to make two more cross stitches in the bottom punched holes.

committed crafter

Cheery banner

WHAT YOU NEED

- ☐ Cotton tote bag
- ☐ 20in (50cm) length of dowelling
- ☐ String
- ☐ Scissors
- ☐ Pencil
- ☐ Assortment of coloured embroidery floss

Not only does this project remind you just how remarkable you are but it also makes a lovely decorative feature to brighten up any lacklustre wall space. With the base made from an old cotton tote, it's a contemporary wall hanging and also a cheeky upcycle.

1 Unpick the stitching where the bag handles are attached to the tote bag and discard them.

2 Using your scissors, cut along all the edges of the tote bag so you are left with two single rectangular pieces of fabric with hems at the top.

3 Either draw your message freestyle on your bag or type your word in large letters, print it out, draw round the letters in pencil and then transfer to the bag by drawing over the back of the paper so that the pencil marks transfer onto the bag.

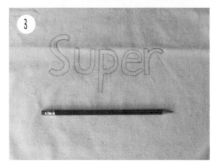

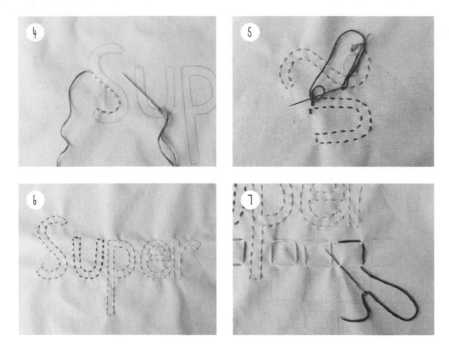

Tip! With practice you can stitch all sorts of messages and greetings to inspire and uplift you.

4 Thread the needle with a 6in (15cm) length of embroidery floss, tie a knot in the end and, starting from the back of the fabric, sew the outline of the 'S' using a small running stitch (see page 20). Finish at the back of the fabric and sew in the ends.

5 Thread the needle with a different coloured length of embroidery floss and sew the outline of the next letter, making sure you finish at the back of the fabric and sew in the ends.

6 Repeat for each of the letters in a selection of your favourite colours.

7 Now embroider squares in different colours, using a long running stitch for each side. Start in the top left-hand corner and work round in a clockwise direction. Finish the ends on the back of the fabric.

8 Starting at the centre of the bottom edge of your fabric, cut from the middle upwards at an angle.

9 This will create a pointed end at the bottom of your banner.

10 Now thread the length of dowelling along the top of the tote through the existing hemmed edge.

11 Cut a length of string approximately 12in (30cm) long and tie it onto each end of the piece of dowelling.

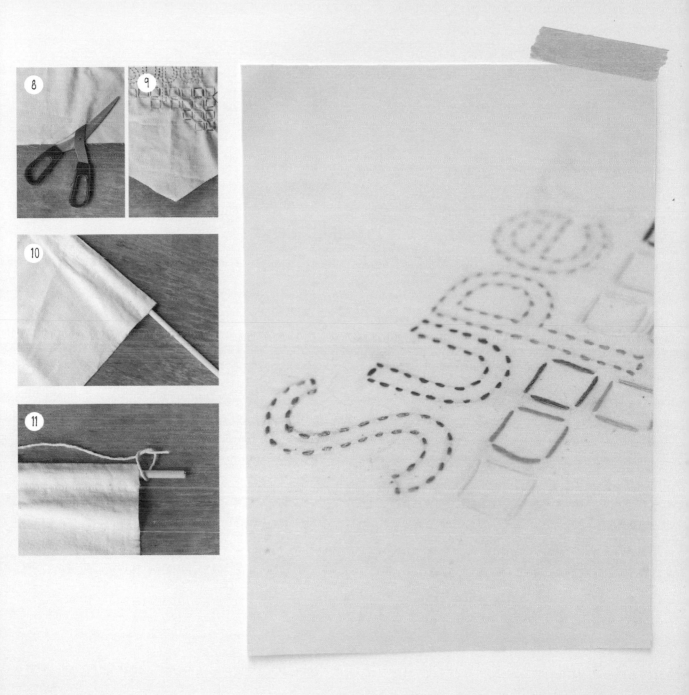

Cross-stitch chair

Here's a revamp project with a cross-stitch twist. Unlike your average cross-stitch sampler, at the end of this step-by-step you will have an on-trend statement piece of furniture to brighten your space.

WHAT YOU NEED

- ☐ Old cane chair
- ☐ Blue, pink and yellow embroidery floss
- ☐ Needle
- ☐ Scissors or a seam ripper
- ☐ Superglue

1 Cut a length of blue embroidery floss approximately 24in (60cm) long and thread your needle. Start by coming up on the far right of the cane, making sure to leave a 4in (10cm) strand at the bottom. Work along the chair, sewing your first diagonal lines.

2 Once you get to the end of the row, go back on yourself to complete the row of cross stitch (see page 27).

3 Repeat lines of this colour until you have competed five rows of cross stitch.

Tip! Due to the stiffness of the cane and the spacing, it is not possible to tie knots as you go along. If any of the ends aren't automatically stitched in as you are going along you can superglue them at the end.

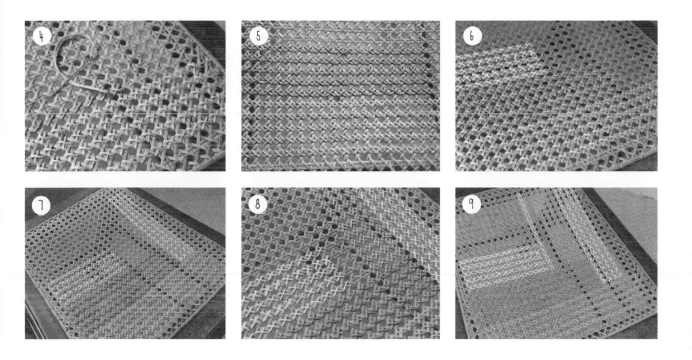

4 Thread your needle with a long length of pink embroidery floss. Starting from the left-hand side, stitch your diagonal lines but this time stop six stitches short of the edge of the blue stitches. When you reach this point, turn back on yourself to complete the row of cross stitch.

5 Repeat to the same point four more times until you have five pink rows.

6 Now stitch five rows of yellow cross stitches, starting level with the pink rows at the left but stopping six stitches sooner.

7 Now starting in the corner above the blue stitches and next to the pink ones, add a column of yellow cross stitches, stopping the same distance from the back of the chair as the first blue row was from the front. Add three more yellow columns.

8 To the left of the yellow columns add a blue one, starting above the pink rows and stopping the same distance from the back of the chair as the yellow columns. Add three more blue columns to the left of this.

9 To the left of this, stitch a column of pink embroidery cross stitches, then a column of yellow cross stitches next to that. Complete the pattern with four columns of pink stitches, starting above the first yellow panel and ending the same distance from the back of the chair as the other columns. Turn the chair over to finish off the ends. Some of your stray ends will have been sewn in as you have been going along. Dab a bit of superglue underneath any loose ends, leave for a few seconds and push the thread down to secure. Leave to dry for a few hours then trim them as close as possible.

Cactus sampler

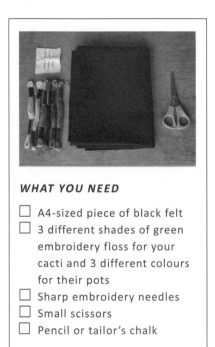

WHAT YOU NEED

- [ ] A4-sized piece of black felt
- [ ] 3 different shades of green embroidery floss for your cacti and 3 different colours for their pots
- [ ] Sharp embroidery needles
- [ ] Small scissors
- [ ] Pencil or tailor's chalk

For a contemporary take on a timeless favourite, why not give our cacti mixed-stitch sampler a go? Playing around with stitch combinations and colours is a fantastic way to get to grips with traditional embroidery and also build up the confidence to freestyle your own designs.

1   Trace the template (see page 114) onto a sheet of paper. Turn it over and draw over the back of the design with tailor's chalk.

2   Now place the paper chalk side down on the felt and using a blunt pencil draw firmly over the design to transfer the chalk to the felt.

3   You will now have a chalk outline to follow on the felt. Begin work on the left-hand cactus. Start by embroidering the outline of the pot in backstitch (see page 21).

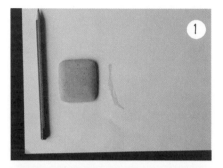

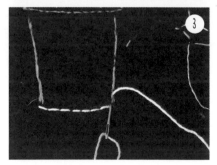

Tip! Work each cactus motif as a separate project to keep your work focused and manageable.

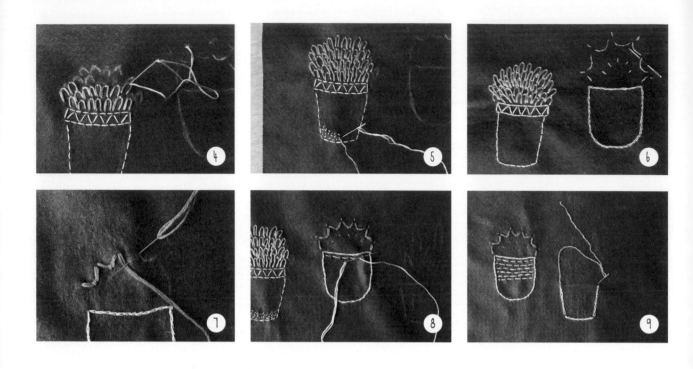

4 Embellish the top of the pot with zigzags. Then using lots of single chain stitches (see page 22) add the cactus prongs, working from left to right and letting your plant grow organically.

5 Add detail to the bottom of the pot with seed stitch (see page 21).

6 Moving on to the middle cactus, embroider the outline of the pot in split stitch (see page 25).

7 Now use scalloping chain stitch (see page 23) to add your cactus plant.

8 Finish cactus number two using running stitch (see page 20) to add detail to the top of the pot. Add accents to the plant using seed stitch.

9 Begin cactus three by embroidering the pot outline in chain stitch. Stitch the top of the pot with one long running stitch.

10 Use scalloping chain stitch for the cactus leaves.

11 Add detail with small cross stitches (see page 27).

12 Finish by adding detail to the pot with a chain-stitch spray (page 24).

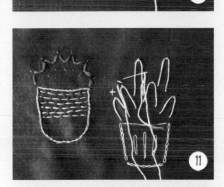

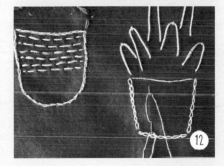

Tip! Once the embroidery is complete frame and hang above your desk or crafting spot to remind you of the many stitches used in the motif, and to water your plants!

COSY EAR MUFFS, PAGE 80

Stylishly stitched sweater

WHAT YOU NEED

- ☐ Sweater, preferably in cotton sportswear or thick jersey fabric
- ☐ Needles
- ☐ An assortment of odds and ends of coloured threads
- ☐ Tailor's chalk
- ☐ Pins
- ☐ Iron

With a nod to all things folksy, this gorgeous sweater update is worth whiling away a few hours on. The heavily embellished yoke detail is a great project for using up that treasure trove of leftover ends and offcuts of floss that as we all know can gather up easily.

1 Using the rib of the neck trim as a guide for spacing, cross stitch (see page 27) around the neck opening.

2 Using satin stitch (see page 28), cover the hem of the neck trim in blocks of colour of random lengths.

3 Repeat with a second row of random-length coloured stitching below your first. This second row will be more difficult as you are working directly onto the sweater now with no seams to guide your stitching.

Tip! Vary your stitch detail by splitting the strand of floss to one or two threads thick for the cross stitch and running stitch details.

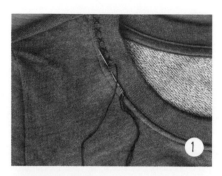

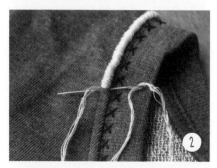

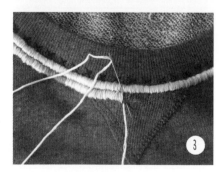

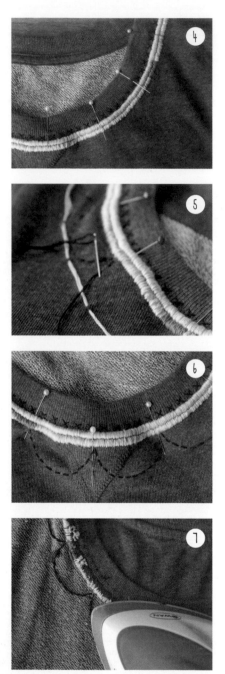

4 You can use pins to plot the scallop design before you begin stitching. This will prove super helpful for achieving equal spacing. Place the pins at regular intervals along the stitching you have already done. This will show where the tops of the semi-circles will go.

5 Using a single strand of thread, mark in running stitch (see page 20) a curve about 1in (2.5cm) below your neck-trim stitching. This will act as a guide to where the bottom of your scalloped pattern will sit. Then, using this line and the pins as a guide, sew the scalloped pattern in a simple running stitch, curving up and down. It helps to draw the curves with tailor's chalk to guide you.

6 Continue to sew the scalloped pattern right round to the other shoulder of the sweater.

7 Take the pins out and press with a steam iron from the inside of the sweater to flatten the satin stitch.

Tip! Trim all finished ends down to a few millimetres after sewing them off securely as you go along. Having so many colour changes will mean tangled ends!

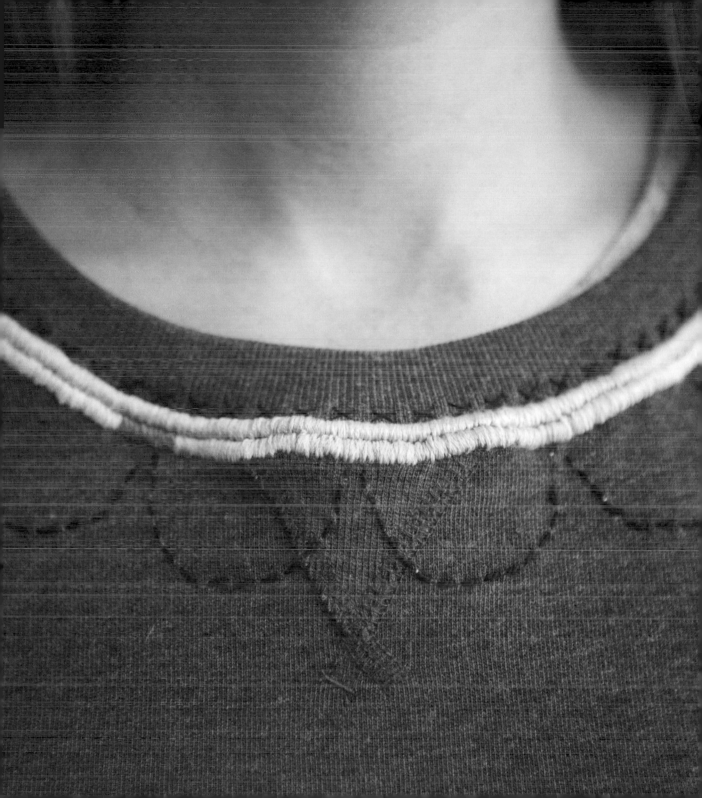

Varsity hoodie

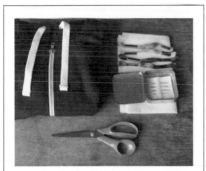

WHAT YOU NEED

- [ ] Zipped hooded top
- [ ] Iron-on stiffening fabric
- [ ] Tracing paper
- [ ] 4 different colours of embroidery floss
- [ ] Pencil
- [ ] Scissors
- [ ] Iron
- [ ] Embroidery needle

This step-by-step is the perfect project for sharing and fighting over who's wearing! Decide on an initial and away you go. If sharing's not your thing it might make a super birthday present instead.

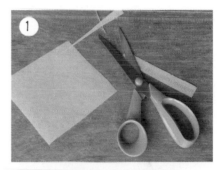

1   Draw your design onto tracing paper with pencil using the design on page 115 as a guide. If your initial is not symmetrical you will need to make it a mirror image. Cut a square of the stiffening fabric a bit bigger than your design.

2   Copy the template onto the stiffening fabric by putting the tracing paper pencil side down and drawing over the back. Set the temperature on your iron to medium and press the fabric onto the inside of the hoodie where you want your motif to go.

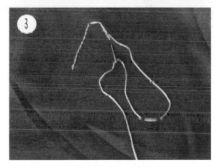

3   Thread your needle with a 12in (30cm) length of embroidery floss and tie a knot in the end. Push the needle from the inside of the hoodie through to the front. Embroider the outline of the initial using long split stitches (see page 25).

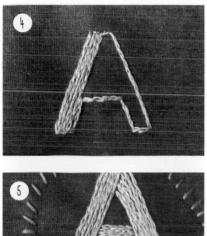

4 Fill in the lines using split stitch too.

5 Thread your needle with a 12in (30cm) length of different coloured embroidery floss and sew an over stitch border (see page 26) around your letter. Leave a gap at the top and bottom of the circle.

6 Change to another colour of embroidery floss for the bottom stitches in this border and the backstitch (see page 21) and cross stitch (see page 27) combo at the top of the motif.

7 Complete the design by using another colour of embroidery floss and adding another three cross stitches inside the bottom circle of the motif.

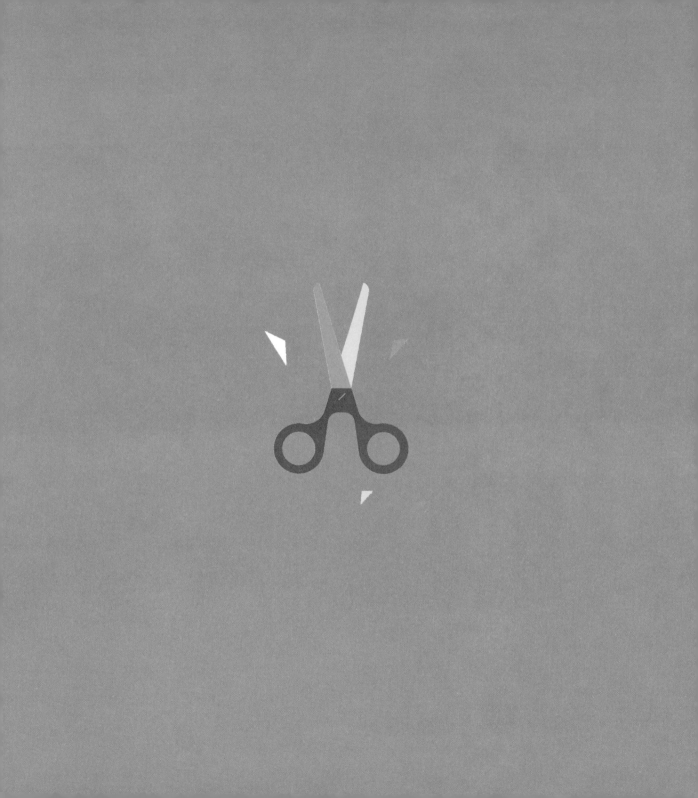

...... **bits and bobs** ......

Templates

Use these designs as inspiration or copy them free hand.
You can also transfer the design by tracing it in pencil onto
tracing paper, positioning the paper face down on your
project and drawing over the back. With patterns involving
lettering you will need to redraw it on the reverse side and
place that side on your project to make sure your design
is not the wrong way round.

Penny wren purse, page 82.
Copy this at a size to fit your purse.

Folksy bib collar, page 62.
Copy this at 100% or adapt
to fit your shirt.

Cosy ear muffs, page 80.
Copy this at a size to fit your ear muffs.

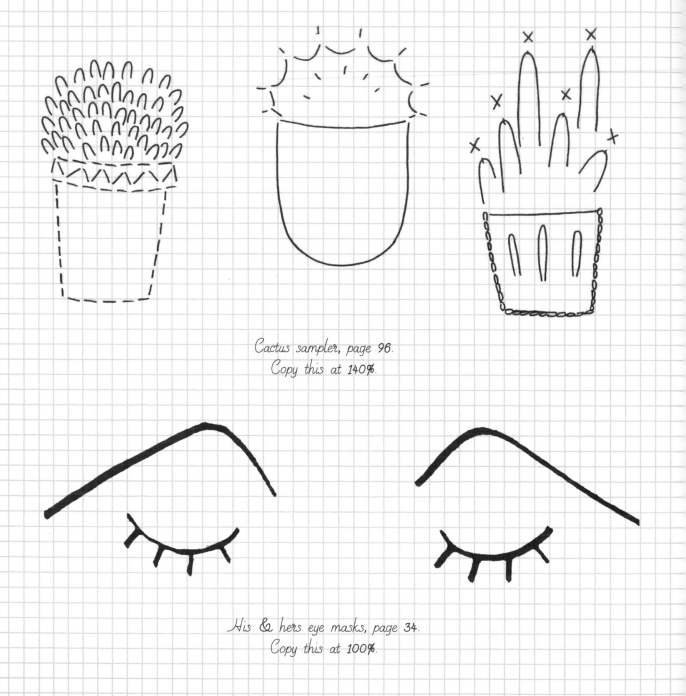

Cactus sampler, page 96.
Copy this at 140%.

His & hers eye masks, page 34.
Copy this at 100%.

Jazzy tablet case, page 84.
Copy this at 100% or adapt to fit your case.

Varsity hoodie, page 106.
Copy this at 100% or adapt
with your own initial.

Animal door stop, page 76.
Copy this at 100%.

Resources

supplies

Ardingly Antiques Fair
www.iacf.co.uk/Ardingly

ArtiFolk
www.artifolk.co.uk

C & H Fabrics
www.candh.co.uk

The Eternal Maker
www.eternalmaker.com

Etsy
www.etsy.com

Fabric Land
www.fabricland.co.uk

Hobbycraft
www.hobbycraft.co.uk

John Lewis
www.johnlewis.com

Not on the High Street
www.notonthehighstreet.com

events

Creative Stitches & Hobbycrafts
www.ichfevents.co.uk

The Knitting & Stitching Show
www.theknittingandstitchingshow.com

Made Brighton
www.brighton-made.co.uk

Top Drawer London
www.topdrawer.co.uk

inspiration

Anthropology
www.anthropologie.eu

Belle Armoire
www.bellearmoire.com

Cloth House
www.clothhouse.com

Craftgawker
craftgawker.com

Hand & Lock
www.handembroidery.com

Karen Barbé
www.karenbarbe.com

Kinfolk
www.kinfolk.com

Mister Finch
www.mister-finch.com

Oh Comely
www.ohcomely.co.uk

Acknowledgements

To the many friends, family members and loved ones who have come and gone through the whirlwind that is setting up your own business, we want to say thank you. Without you we would not have stuck at this, our dream project. It would be unfair to name a special few people as there are so many that have been involved and inspired us, so we'd like to say thank you for friendship. Because that inevitably is what it always comes back to. We'd also like to thank everyone at GMC for believing in our brand.

Index

A
Animal door stop 76–9, 116

B
backstitch 21
Birdhouse picture 54–9

C
Cactus sampler 96–9, 114
calico 19
chain stitch 22
chain stitch spray 24
Cheery banner 88–91
Chill-out slippers 50–1
Cosy ear muffs 80–1, 113
couching 28
crewels 15
cross stitch 27
Cross-stitch chair 92–5

D
damask 19
diagonal straight stitch 26

E
embroidery floss 19
embroidery hoops 16
embroidery thread 19

F
fabrics 19
Fancy elbow pads 32–3
Festival shorts 48–9
floss 19
Folksy bib collar 62–5, 112
French knot 25

G
Geometric phone case 44–7
Glammed-up gloves 42–3

H
His & hers eye masks 34–5, 114
hoops 16

I
Ikat-style cushion 70–3

I
Japanese screw punch 16
Jazzy tablet case 84–5, 115
jersey 19

L
leatherwork needles 15

M
machine thread 19
masking tape 16
metallic thread/floss 19

N
needles 15

O
over stitch 26

P
paper 16
pencils 16
pens 16
pinking shears 15
pins 15

R
running stitch 20

S
satin stitch 28
scalloping chain stitch 23
scissors 15
seed stitch 21
sharps 15
Silhouette napkins 38–9
snips 15
split stitch 25
staggered chain stitch 23
steel ruler 16
stem stitch 29
sticky tape 16
Stylishly stitched sweater 102–5

T
tailor's chalks 16
tape measures 16
templates 112–16
thread 19
tracing paper 16

V
Varsity hoodie 106–9, 115
Vintage tray cloth curtain 66–9

W
washing embroidery 19
Wren penny purse 82–3, 112

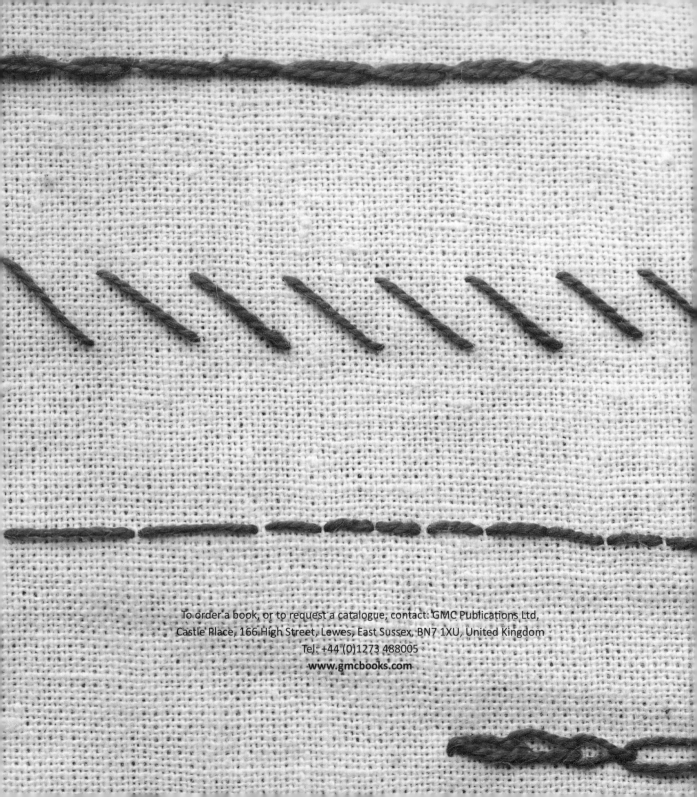

To order a book, or to request a catalogue, contact: GMC Publications Ltd,
Castle Place, 166 High Street, Lewes, East Sussex, BN7 1XU, United Kingdom
Tel: +44 (0)1273 488005
www.gmcbooks.com